SHAPING DESTINY

A quest for meaning in art and life

By

DESTINY ALLISON

ISBN: 1468077333
ISBN-13: 9781468077339

Library of Congress Control Number: 2011963101
CreateSpace, North Charleston, SC

For Steve, because there will never be enough words.
And for my sons, may the journey be enough.

AUTHOR'S NOTE

This book is my journey through life and art. Names have been changed and some of the narrative has been slightly fictionalized. In addition, it is important to note that the stories I tell are from my memories. Many of them are from my childhood and reflect the perspective of a very young mind. Consequently, my recounting of events does not necessarily imply factual occurrences. In fact, several of the stories I tell here have later proved to be incorrect. Still, these memories shaped me and became my touchstones. Their purpose in the book is to inform the journey and move it forward.

Shaping Destiny is a complex composition of experience, ideas and emotions. Narrated through three distinct voices, it attempts to reveal the creative process in depth and illuminate the transformative power of art.

The teaching voice serves as a guide. The lessons preceding each chapter can be taken literally or metaphorically and applied to both art and life. The emotional voice is raw, personal, and frequently charged as it reacts to life experiences. The intellectual voice examines those experiences and processes them analytically to draw conclusions and create order. Having never been to art school, or taken an art class, some of the terminologies I use are my interpretations of things I discovered or made up along the way.

I believe that art and self awareness are enhanced by the dialog between the teaching, intellectual and emotional voices. Developing them and giving them strength – through introspection, education, and expression – is the primary job of the artist and the crux of the creative process.

Art is about more than materials and technique. It is about giving shape and form to who we are and how we see the world.

Lesson 1

There are only two rules for any artistic process. The first is that we must choose a subject that matters to us, a subject that we care about on an intensely personal level. We cannot copy someone else's concept or borrow an emotion. The second rule is that we must be open to criticism and participate in the discussion. By doing so, we gain insight about others and ourselves, as well as the language and power of art.

CHAPTER 1

Night was when my lack of voice was most apparent. It was then, during silent moments, void of chaos, that I realized I did not know myself. I could not speak or write. My desire to give form to my ideas of love and marriage caused me to gift my very essence to a man before I even knew what it was. Imprisoned by my choice, I couldn't breathe.

My husband and I were fighting. He was in one room studying for a promotion he didn't want, and I was in another trying to write. But I was unable to express the picture in my mind. A lump of clay was on my desk, a crude reminder of my hectic day with my children. It was soft, Plasticine clay used by children and hobbyists. Taking it in my hands, I made a tiny figurine of a grotesquely pregnant woman. She was disproportionate. Her arched back barely compensated for the hard, swollen mass that was her belly. I folded her legs in a sitting position and wrapped long, worm-like arms underneath her stomach so I would not have to model tiny hands. The figure had holes for eyes and a mask-like face. I could not make her hair look natural, so I crowned her with a wreath and she became regal in spite of the fact that she was only five inches tall. She reminded me of my own pregnancies. She was not glowing or holy. Instead, she appeared tired and resigned. Her face looked up, away from her baby, and her gaze was direct, not dreamy. I knew she would endure this pregnancy and not get lost in motherhood as I had. She would keep her identity intact, even as her shape shifted and grew.

I rolled the sticky, brown clay between my fingers, feverishly smoothing and pressing little pieces onto the form. I forgot about my husband in the other room, the children sleeping above me, the desk in need of tidying, and the wood floor requiring care. The only thing that mattered was the clay before me because in it, I felt a hunger for something more than I had ever known.

The creation of that first sculpture was cathartic. It was the first time I had considered what it meant to be a woman, the conflict between what I was expected to be, feel, and do, and what I wanted to be, feel, and do. It opened the door to who I am instead of who I was supposed to be, but I didn't recognize the opening. I only knew that I was dissatisfied, that I needed more time and more clay.

Over the course of a year, between diaper changes and trips to the park, building Lego towers and singing children to sleep, money struggles, and impersonal sex, I made tiny women. They were the symbols of all the things I was supposed to be because they were graceful and small, pregnant or submissive. They were terrible sculptures – little Plasticine or self-hardening clay figurines – but they taught me how to give to myself.

Before becoming engaged with sculpture, I wanted to be something more than the person I knew as myself. That had seemed possible only through my relationships with others. As a wife, I was not alone. I belonged to someone and I belonged to the world around me. Marriage was my rite of passage. It validated that I was desirable, respectable, and had something to offer. Motherhood proved I had a purpose in life. I could comfort the tears of my children, elicit their giggles, and answer their questions. They trusted and needed me. The gift of a dandelion and a sloppy, wet kiss from one of my toddlers on a summer afternoon gave me a reason for being I hadn't previously been able to find.

After the birth of my third child, there wasn't always time for dandelions. I seldom had the patience to find the missing toy or play monster on demand. There were sticky marks on my walls from dirty, reaching fingers because cleaning up after the new baby took precedence. My once immaculate house was exhibiting signs of my exhaustion and so was my marriage. In the nursery, I sometimes cried as I tried to rock my baby to sleep. He was the only one who didn't mind my tears. I wanted a break. I wanted to remember what it felt like to live according to the dictates of my desires instead of the demands of my family. I had believed my family would give me substance and importance. I was wrong. I was discovering that I mattered to me.

Sculpture was showing me another way of looking at the world and understanding myself within it. I began to put my needs first. I often said "no" to my children when they persisted in wanting to go to the beach or the park. I rejected my husband's ideal of a woman in waiting – freshly showered and dressed in lingerie – when he came home from work. It was the year I first cooked Thanksgiving dinner because I was no longer willing to eat my mother-in-law's canned green beans and Butterball turkey. I developed a taste for scotch and freshly ground coffee.

For lack of professional sculpting tools, I made do with household objects. I discovered that a manicure tool could shape an eye. I found new uses for old toothbrushes. Besides scrubbing around the sink with them, they could clean up the mottled texture on a new sculpture. A lobster pick was perfect for carving hair. Scouring pads could sand the surface of a sculpted breast so smooth that it gleamed in the light. Everything went through a transformation. My office became a studio. The computer was moved to the bedroom and I stopped caring about the clay shavings that stuck to the floor and the leather surface of my desk. My children learned how to play without me more often because Mommy needed her own time. Each time I worked on a new figure I seized upon something new about myself.

The first sculpture taught me that I could survive pregnancy and birth with my identity intact. Through the second, I realized I was bored because the figure looked bored in her posturing, similar to when I posed in lingerie for my husband. In another sculpture, I recognized that I was holding something inside me because the hunched figure had her arms wrapped around her knees, creating a wall around her body. Despite a face that appeared inviting, nothing could get in. The sculptures became the joy of my life because each created stillness or a pause. When confronted by the implacable idea of woman, time would stop. I wanted to know about being a woman and hold that stillness in myself.

I knew a sculpture was done when I wanted to throw it against the wall and destroy it. When it came to a moment between what I saw and was capable of rendering, I would paint it, put it on a shelf and start again – a new woman, small enough to hold in the palm of my hand, awkward, stiff and evolving. I too was evolving and learning again how to breathe. At the end of that first year, seven tiny figures stood on a shelf. Then I hit a wall and didn't know where to turn.

Learning about the history of sculpture or even looking at another artist's work scared me. I thought that if I saw or knew more about sculpture than what I was personally experiencing, in some way the development of my own voice would be compromised. I wanted to hold my discovery like a treasure, like the first week of falling in love when feelings are fragile yet all-consuming, when love can only be felt through touch and holding, and truly known only by engaging and giving everything. In love with my work, I was blind and consequently frustrated.

Lacking the anatomical knowledge or the manipulative skill to express what I wanted through the female figure, I thought about body language. I wanted proof that what I perceived in other people's gestures was real, not the fabric of my insecurity and imagination. I hung mirrors around my desk to watch my sculpture and myself while I worked. Posing naked, I tried to understand expression through the positioning of my body. When something in my body belied the expression on my face, hundreds of questions arose. I wanted to know why people smiled when their body suggested anger or sadness. I didn't understand how figures of authority could issue commands when their bodies were hunched over and their movements were slow. When put to others, these questions made people angry, but they were somehow drawn to the truth I was seeking and, in turn, wanted to hold my sculptures. I came out of that first year knowing that faces can lie but bodies do not and that I loved being a woman.

Wanting to know more about my relationships, my roles, and myself, I began working on a new piece. This sculpture began as a single figure and was larger than any of the others. But there were difficulties with it I hadn't yet encountered. The clay didn't want to stand up. It kept slipping down and falling on top of itself. I incorporated another figure for balance and added strength by wiring the two figures together. It was wonderful to slide my hands up and down the length of these forms and because of the larger scale, I could move freely as I worked around the piece. I did not have to hunch over and use tiny tools. I dared to close my eyes while I worked. The wet clay was slippery and sensual as it coated my fingers and the palms of my hands. I opened my eyes, and the clay was glistening and white.

The form began to take shape. I made a male and a female figure intertwined and didn't worry about detail or anatomy. I wanted to keep my hands moving. Needing more height and length, I added more clay to the bottom, giving me the freedom to stroke and roam. The bodies reminded me of a vine, twisted and coiled, so I worked with that feeling – letting it dictate the form. The figures evolved as half human, half flower, and all sex. I glanced in my mirror, trying to see two sides of the piece simultaneously and was startled to find a cow skull in the reflection. It was a skeletal form created by the woman's back and the man's legs and intertwined with the vine-like form from which both figures grew. Needing to verify what I saw, I turned the piece around and touched it. It was real. Death appeared in my sculpture, a sculpture that I thought was solely about love and life. I worked harder on developing the skull than I did the figures, and *Blue Night Smoke* became my first abstraction.

As I worked on this sculpture, images flashed in my head. I remembered visiting relatives in Alabama the summer after my father died. I had snuck out of the house to get away from the mildew, clutter, and conciliatory voices that wrapped around me like the vegetation – cloying and damp. I wanted a cigarette. In the park down the road, I met a boy on a swing who was smoking a joint. His voice was deep with Southern drawl and his touch was intentional. We kissed in the suffocating air. He laid me down against the edge of the grass where the smell of green and rot from the nearby vines made me gasp. Writhing and twisting, my body arched to meet his. I was fourteen – still a virgin – and was afraid to let things go further. Our breathing cooled and the night came back. Walking home, instead of feeling like I had done the right thing, I longed for what might have happened. Something needed to die that night, to be crushed under his weight, but I didn't take the risk.

It seemed *Blue Night Smoke* was trying to teach me something. Why else would these memories be surfacing? I was twenty-five, married with three children, and living a long way from Alabama. I felt something tugging at me, a mystery that demanded resolution. I thought I knew about sex. Still, death presented itself in my sculpture and it was more interesting to me than the intertwined bodies that framed it.

Before the birth of my children, sexuality had given me my only real sense of power. When I flaunted it, I felt alive and beautiful. I was in control of the male gaze with my makeup, short skirts and spiked heels. I tilted my head and let my hair fall slightly over my eyes when I spoke to people. I made my eyes flash and knew I could take anyone to bed. Now I didn't do any of those things. Had I lost the power of my sexuality? Had motherhood and marriage transformed me? Was I getting old? The sculpture worried me.

My husband certainly wasn't as interested as he used to be. He had stopped touching me during my first pregnancy. After my twin sons were born and the recovery period over, I asked him to make love to me and he couldn't. He wasn't ready. It took a long time for me to forgive him for that rejection. Sex never returned to the way it had been. I was embarrassed by my body, and my stretch marks made my husband uncomfortable. He didn't like to touch my belly anymore. I blamed myself for what had transpired and felt I had lost a part of my identity. The distortion of my body and my attention to the kids shifted my focus. I didn't always have time to shower or put on my makeup. I couldn't linger in bed before my husband went to work because I couldn't leave the kids unattended. Meeting their needs was my first priority. It seemed that my husband was feeling unimportant and ignored. I made a real effort to lose the baby weight, make myself attractive, and put him first. He did not respond. When I started making art, things got worse.

Then I got angry. I didn't understand why sex between us was limited to my ability to camouflage my stretch marks and quiet the kids. I didn't know why he was the one who controlled when – or if – we made love. I didn't appreciate his lack of respect for my life, or the needs of our children. Sex became urgent. It was like a struggle for dominance that always resulted in me yielding to his wants, his rhythm, and his pace.

Confronting the conflicts in my marriage and myself enabled me to approach the obstacles I was encountering in my work. From between the tangled legs of my sculpture, death stared at me impassively. The cow skull portion of the piece was well defined. I worked again on the bodies, trying to resolve the conflict. I had started this piece wanting to know about my relationship but I moved away from that intent, focusing instead on my own sexuality by working the clay that formed the cow skull. The back of the female figure, including her slender waist and wide hips, was the face of the skull. I turned the piece around and worked on the male figure. I wanted his shoulders to be big and menacing, yet protective. He had to envelop her with his body. His back became fan shaped, similar to the head of a cobra. I looked again at the forms and realized that the sculpture wasn't just about my sexuality. Each of the figures was assuming a role. She was submissive, slick and sensuous. He was strong, powerful and threatening. In short, the piece was more about the roles we assume during sex than the sexuality of the individuals engaged in it.

The act of sex was the one thing in my life not dominated by self-consciousness or fear. I could let go. My husband could not. To him, sex was impersonal, an instinctual craving for something that came and went like hunger, easily soothed, relatively unimportant, and separate from the way he wanted to see himself. He loathed being dirty, but the showers he took following sex could not wash away the memory of the experience, let alone the scent on the sheets or in the room. A cigarette could not soothe his emotional and physical vulnerability after we were done. Nothing but my next cycle could calm his fear of yet another pregnancy.

Sex had been my escape. It was a nonverbal realm that suspended time. Here in this water-like domain, I could fight – with nails, teeth, and an intensity that mimicked passion. I was able to touch, breathe, and feel that I was real. Stretching toward God and not afraid of falling, I was willing to lose myself to find union and, consequently, strength. For me, orgasm was like falling through fire. It jolted me into a way of living that was different, stronger, and more real than my day-to-day life. I had seen glimpses of this way of life when I sculpted and in the books I read. I felt the intensity in music – in traditional jazz, Delta Blues and in the lyrics of Bob Dylan. I had witnessed it in the face of my father when I listened to him talk in the years before his death.

My father spoke of the South, of family, and of blood. Lying on his king-sized bed, staring at the twilight through the skylights in his room, he talked of a world that moved beyond the rancid fear of dry Southern counties – a night-world where blacks sang the Blues and men got shot for acting on their beliefs. He talked of art, literature, and jazz and told me that when I saw beauty in a sunset, it was a reflection of the beauty I saw in myself. His lyrical voice carried me beyond our home in the high, brown desert of New Mexico, beyond my childhood insecurities to places where life was rich and real. I was a child when he romanced me with his words, his voice, and his image of a passionate life. I wanted to experience it for myself, and now my sculpture was showing me how.

Blue Night Smoke depicts the physiological act of a man penetrating a woman and reveals inherent psychological associations. For me, the act of sex was expressed by the age-old metaphor and myth of being stabbed or swallowed whole. Sex was a violent thing. The wrestling, rolling, grunts and near screaming mimicked a brutal fight that ended in surrender. Letting go was kin to death. But sex was also a magic realm, full of softness and grace.

As I completed *Blue Night Smoke*, I saw what I had felt but never spoken. The form of the sculpture was a manifestation of the wriggling, slippery, writhing beauty of life. I saw in it a truth that became a building block for my future. I realized that I was fully alive in the moments where death stared back at me from between tangled legs.

I was in love with sculpture. I loved the physicality of the work and how the act of creation consumed those empty hours after my children had fallen asleep and before my husband would get home from work. Through sculpture, the kind of life my father had described was visible, almost tangible. I had found the value of emotional honesty. I had found a voice.

Lesson 2

Sculpting is learning a new language, a vocabulary that evolves through the use of medium, tools, and the method of creation. The process is physical and requires that we be physical too. The physicality of the work is a vehicle through which we can learn to listen to ourselves.

CHAPTER 2

I had never shown my work to anyone other than family and friends, but after completing *Blue Night Smoke*, I felt I had reached a new level of artistic expression. I wanted to test that notion in the real world, but I knew the piece had to be re-imagined into a fine art medium and bronze seemed to be the only choice. At the time, I had no idea what the "lost wax method" of cast bronze meant. I only knew that it was a process of conversion from a temporary medium into a permanent one. The first bronze foundry I called made screws for ships. When I finally figured out where I was going, I packed the piece in Styrofoam, slipped on my best red dress and drove a hundred miles across a state line with the intent to make my work last. It was everything I could do not to cry when the foundry manager looked at the piece and quoted me $1,200.00 to cast it in bronze. I thought my world had ended. He was not in the market for a secretary and he already had people to sweep the floor, but as I was repacking the piece, he told me to keep working and that I had what it took. I believed him and was ready to learn.

I bought a book on mold making and sought the advice of those who knew how to make flexible molding material out of silicone caulking and gauze bandage. After reading the book, I built a box in which to smother the silicone-covered sculpture in clay and then plaster. In my office – replete with beautiful wood floors and rugs – I poured the plaster into the box and watched in horror as the fluid, white mixture drained through the cracks in the box and ran across the floor, covering everything in its wake. It took three days to get the plaster completed and three days to open the mold when it was cured. I had used more than 150 pounds of plaster for an eight-inch sculpture. By the end of the week, I lost both the mold and the sculpture and threw away the book.

After another year of backaches, burned hands, and exploded wax on the kitchen stove, I became an apprentice at a foundry in Boston. The situation didn't please my family and they expressed their feelings accordingly. My children poked holes in my clay and my husband refused to pay for materials or childcare. I was, in spite of them, resolute. I used and reused materials. I asked for tools for birthdays and Christmas and worked as often as I could. I sang to my children for over an hour every afternoon so that I could steal an hour of work while they napped. With every breath, I inhaled bronze dust until my sinuses bled but only wanted more. I turned my lawn into a wasteland of discarded ceramic shell, plaster, and sand. I learned how to use the proper tools, how to melt metal and transform it, how to mix acids, apply heat, and create color.

I made molds of my sculptures with rubber and plaster. I poured scalding hot wax into those molds and rolled it around, repeatedly coating the inside of the rubber until I could pull out a hollow wax form. I worked the new waxes, re-texturing the surface where the mold had left air bubbles and seam lines. When the waxes were dressed and ready for casting, I made sprues, or wax pipes, so the metal would run freely and quickly without cooling prematurely during the casting phase. At the foundry, I coated the finished waxes with a ceramic shell material that could withstand the heat and pressure of two-thousand-degree metal being poured into them like liquid sun. Then, my foundry team fired the shells, melting out the wax and creating hollow forms that the metal would fill. After the casting, I chipped the vitrified, white shell from the cooled and blackened bronzes. Chasing the metal with hand tools, I worked the pieces until every bubble and every flash of foil-like metal from cracks in the molds were gone to the point where they were smooth and ready to be colored using acids and heat.

I was learning a new language. I was at the core of something ancient and primal. The casting process was more intense than anything I had ever experienced. Fire became a vital tool. I could feel its piercing heat through my protective gear as we poured molten metal just inches from our bodies. If my gloves caught on fire, as they often did, I would have to wait to put them out or lose six weeks of work and preparation. I knew the silent dance after the roar of the furnaces had stopped. Silence was the music that supported the rhythm of my breathing.

Some days, sweat burned my eyes and the grinder whined in my ear. I knew a moment without fight. My colleagues at the foundry valued me for the work I contributed.

My looks, children, and husband were irrelevant in this place. I discovered a power I had never known. My world shifted. Suddenly, I was larger than my past, my family, and who I was supposed to have become. My world could be about questions and without boundaries.

There were four men and two women in that foundry. We were all sculptors, or wanted to be, and we were all thinking about art – what it was and why most of what we saw was not. There was jazz on the stereo, falafels for lunch, and draft Guinness after the pours. During all of it, Rick, the foundry owner, was my mentor. Over the noise of the power tools, in between cups of molding rubber, and after a patina was finished, he would critique my work and demonstrate with other sculptures the concepts he wanted me to grasp.

Rick talked about something I thought I would never understand – sculptural planes. They were a mystery to me. I did not know what he meant when he told me to follow a plane. Given that there were multiple planes to consider, I never knew to which one he was referring. There were concave and convex planes, linear, repetitive, and parallel planes, the planes of each separate mark of texture, and the larger plane of a form that contained a variety of planes in its interior – all of which confused me. But I listened because he was the first man who had ever approached me as a person instead of merely a woman. He was tall and skinny with round glasses and powerful hands. He was naturally inclined as a mechanical engineer and had built the foundry piece by piece – from the furnace and kiln to the rotating tanks that held the slurry of wet ceramic shell. He had worked with some of the best sculptors in the country, built shops for them, designed their tools, and installed their sculptures in public places. He talked constantly about sculpture and showed me books in which pictures of various sculptures made him pause in admiration. Surprisingly, Rick did not sculpt. Instead, he taught me about jazz and Carl Jung and didn't ask about my life. He gave me tools and sent me working until my back ached and my hands were swollen and bleeding. But in the end, I was strong enough to throw a hundred-pound bag of plaster over my shoulder and walk it out to my car. Rick made the foundry a safe place for me.

During my foundry experience, we worked mostly on little statuettes that made learning difficult. But every once in a while, a sculpture would come in that was so beautiful it compelled me to touch it even though I couldn't say why. As my working knowledge of sculpture deepened, my work changed. Through the rubber and plaster process, I learned that every sculpture has a basic form. Through wax dressing and metal chasing, I learned how detail serves to enhance that form. I learned the value of texture, as well as the nuance of line, shape, light and shadow. Indeed, texture is an extension of the form because it recreates the feel of the form in the body of a work. Then something shot me forward, rocked me, and made me reach. I was asked to teach an adult sculpture class at a little museum on the Massachusetts/Rhode Island border.

Lesson 3

An armature is like a skeleton. It is an underlying framework that supports muscle and movement in a sculpture. It is important to understand this, for once the clay is built upon the armature, one has little leeway in varying from the original design. If the design is flawed, so, too, will be the sculpture.

CHAPTER 3

I don't know why the museum hired me. I had only six completed bronze sculptures and one small gallery in Maine that represented my work. I had no real qualifications. I knew little about art history, let alone sculpting techniques. I had never attended a formal sculpting class and I had no idea what I was going to teach these people.

Rick gave me his college assignments and I studied them. They were a series of exercises designed to teach balance, the variety of planes, and craftsmanship. They helped me to verbalize my understanding of planes and to affirm that I had no business teaching this course.

I went to the art department at a nearby college and asked to see their slide library. Exploring the sculpture section helped me to recognize the works by artists to whom I had been compared. I looked up the definition of sculpture in the dictionary. Sculpture came from the root *sculpere* – to carve or alter. There was also a reference to the term "shelf" in the dictionary and when I looked it up something clicked. I imagined an ocean shelf, carved and altered by the shifting sea. I thought about myself, about how I had been carved and altered by the shifting of my life. I knew I was subject to the impact of my experiences and that sculpting increased my awareness of that impact, causing my perceptions to shift.

This was a start. But I didn't think I could teach students how to express it or learn from it. I worked with what I knew about sculpture – it had mass, volume and was three-dimensional.

I understood mass to be the basic form, the basic shape. As I thought about the shape, I realized that there were five basic shapes represented in all of the sculpture I had seen. I wondered if that meant anything significant.

I believed that body language could inspire a predictable emotional response, so I set up a test. I took the basic shape of each one of my sculptures and drew the shape on a piece of paper. Then I wrote sequential directives at the top of the page:

> *For each shape think of an object in the world that has this shape.*
> *Think of an action associated with your object.*
> *Think of an emotion associated with your action.*
> *Write down your answers.*

I gave the test to my husband and his response to each shape was what I had wanted to convey in each of the sculptures. I had discovered something. I gave the test to everyone I knew and every time the results were the same. The only variations were in object association. Some people said the triangle reminded them of a pyramid, some a mountain. The emotional response was unilateral. For each shape there were only two possible interpretations.

Triangle: *The most common interpretation is emotion associated with joyous attainment. It has elements of spirituality, individual action, and hope. The second interpretation is emotion associated with danger, such as fear, anger, and control. The triangle is a power symbol. It is one of high action and denotes cause and effect.*

Circle: *The most common interpretation is emotion associated with jubilant motion. It is high energy and often dizzying in effect. The second interpretation involves meditation, completion, and life cycles. The circle is also a power symbol and highly active.*

Oval: *The oval is always associated with vulnerability and the process of becoming. It is most often positive, associated with new life or growth. It can also be negative, associated with pain and grief.*

Square and Rectangle: *These shapes are interchangeable and the interpretation is personal. If an individual believes that the boundaries of the rectangle promote feelings of safety and security, then that individual will associate the square with entrapment. Both shapes can be comforting and nurturing or threatening and scary. Both are solid and static.*

I was elated. All my life I had been caught up in the debate over the definition of art. I could never resign myself to the idea that art is subjective, its quality determined only by individual taste. I knew that it was more, but I had never been able to explain why. With this geometric language I had a way in, the start of an explanation.

I now began to examine sculpture with a critical eye. The work I liked had clarity, basic form, and conviction. A triangle was clearly a triangle. An oval form was clearly oval. Other work had things out of place – the basic form was confusing because a shoulder was too high or a leg was opened too far. There was no way to emotionally respond to a work that didn't meet the shape criteria. Then I read something about the sculptor Rodin. In his work, he had incorporated more muscles than the human body possessed yet the Ecole des Beaux-Arts in Paris had refused to admit him because they thought he was doing body casts. How could Rodin be both convincing and anatomically incorrect? It was simple. He complied with shape. His effusive style allowed him to execute shape with authority. His figures conveyed the human experience, not because they were perfect copies of the human body, but because they were speaking the language of shape, which we understand intrinsically.

As I read, studied and perused galleries and museums in support of my shape theory, I noticed that all good work is comprised of two basic shapes from this core group of five. In sculpture, each pair of shapes works together to express an experience and those expressions mimic body language. Body language is the physical manifestation of experience. It is the first expression and the first method of communication. Through body language, we understand each other.

We know when someone is scared. Their body stiffens and becomes shielded by a gesture of crossed arms and straight legs. We know when that fear is defensive because the legs are spread, the neck is rigid, and the chin is tilted upward. And we know when that fear is dangerous, compelling the person in fear to act, to be the aggressor – arms open up, a foot is set forward, and the body tightens. What I saw when I looked at myself in a mirror was different. It was the fear of vulnerability. My reflection revealed hunched shoulders and a curved back – an oval. My legs were spread, my hands covered my stomach, and my head was straight – a triangle. I saw fear – fear of failure, fear of retribution, and fear of success – but I also saw growth. I was growing beyond my fear and toward an apex of self and solitude by choice. My body spoke the oval of becoming. It spoke the triangle of hope and determination. I read fear written in rigid lines of muscles and bones – clenched jaw and tight hips. I understood the gesture and nuance of body language because it was my gesture, my body language.

Like my body, the work to which I responded had a primary and a secondary shape. The primary shape spoke the experience and the emotion. It was the thing that drew me to a particular piece because I could identify with the emotional symbolism. Triangles and ovals were the shapes I liked best because both spoke to my emotional journey. When I saw a sculpture with a triangular or ovoid form, I wanted to approach it, to know what the piece could reveal about me.

Secondary shapes conveyed an idea – the intellectual response to an emotional experience. A work that had an oval as its primary shape and a square as a secondary shape reminded me that while metamorphosis could occur through a process of becoming, mortality was inescapable and my process would be forever limited by it. When a rectangle was the secondary shape, I could recognize that the walls of my experience provided a safe shelter in which the metamorphosis could occur.

I played with body language and it horrified my husband. I sculpted writhing, twisted forms. I used him as a model and sculpted the way he looked after sex when he turned over and lingered to light a cigarette, his back like a long, curved wall that blocked me from entering. The sculpture was an oval in almost every dimension and it pulled into itself, grieving. I called it *Spent*. And though it was not easily recognizable as a human form, it did have a penis, which was flaccid and small.

My husband thought everyone would recognize the sculpture as him. I thought they wouldn't because no one else saw him curve away from me in bed. They didn't see his fear of being out of control, or how he gathered himself with slow, deep breaths punctuated by the exhalation of smoke that spiraled up into the light of the lamp next to the bed. Outside our home, people saw a big, tall man who hunched a little and grew his belly to balance the power of his frame. They saw a man with kind brown eyes and a child's smile, a balding head and sloppy shoes – kind of sweet and goofy like a big teddy bear. I knew that face lied. I knew that the hunching body and sloppiness were about a man out of place inside himself and hiding something. I knew the transformation that could occur when the little control he possessed began to waver and fear took over, becoming dangerous.

Body language and sculptural language are the same. But with my husband, I recognized that his face and body spoke two seemingly irreconcilable truths about his nature. When I sculpted his long, beautiful back turned away from me, I became aware of the thing I most feared about him. Until that moment, I had repressed my fear and parceled out only the knowledge of him that served my immediate needs. I thought about *Blue Night Smoke* and the awakening I experienced when I discovered that my knowledge didn't come solely from what I thought or what I felt. It came from the synthesis of the two through association and consequent expression. I thought I was sculpting life and love, but I saw death in my sculpture through the spontaneous appearance of a cow skull. I had to explore the relationship between these ideas and come to terms with the fact that in both sculpture and life, conflicting perceptions coexist in the same space.

Through the sculptural process, a personal dialogue occurred that culminated in new understanding. As a woman, I was led to believe in the necessity of submission to men and had understood that giving in was the vehicle through which women might arrive at their desired destination. One could be safe, be loved, and could belong. On a deeper level, I had also known that my need to give in was an excuse for giving up and that my understanding of myself as a woman was only part of who I was.

Finally, I understood that sculpture, like sex, occupies space and suspends time. But it does more. It freezes the moment of conflict and illuminates the battle of self. Sculpture is a mirror that casts a shadow – a dark reflection that exists independently in the world and in its own physical form. There was no mistaking the inherent symbolism in each piece. Sculpture spoke a language I could define and document. I knew then that the language of sculpture is the language of geometric symbolism. It is the language of body and the language of the physical world.

Lesson 4

When we look at an armature, we need to visualize a geometric shape that surrounds the skeletal form. This shape determines the basic mood of the sculpture. Within the sculpture, there is a set of points that parallel the external geometric shape as they are connected through space. Those points might consist of the hipbone and the knee, or the iliac crest and the clavicle. These are reference points. They serve to establish a flow line that acts as a guide for when we get blocked or lose our way during the creative process. We need to protect those reference points as we sculpt.

CHAPTER 4

I was terrified the first night of my class. The fluorescent lighting poorly illuminated a badly marred, white linoleum floor. Storage shelves were piled high with green ceramics, papier-mâché creations done by children, and stacks of old newspapers. Eight women and two men sat silently around a large, rectangular table. I imagined my students would be angry because they had come to learn sculpture technique, not sculptural theory. I believed they wanted practical application, not ideas, and the only thing I had to teach were my convictions.

Almost immediately, I spoke too quickly and felt breathless. I gave them the shape test and predicted their answers. I gave them clay and told them to make abstract sculptures that depicted one of five emotions by using only two shapes. We critiqued the sculptures and guessed the emotion each had chosen. I showed them how they would have been more effective if they had articulated the shapes more clearly or put them in different positions. There was energy and excitement in the room.

We talked about mass and I had them draw an imaginary line around each reference point on a sculpture. From this imaginary line, students learned how mass – the form prior to detail or definition – connects to the base of the sculpture to reveal a shape. By looking at the basic shape of each sculpture, we could see that one student's sculpture of a cat was an oval while another student's sculpture of a woman was a rectangle. The basic shape revealed the emotional symbolism inherent in each form.

As the class progressed, we moved from mass to volume and I went back to the dictionary. The root of volume is *volumen*, or roll. I liked that correlation and I liked that the word volume had something in it that sounded like the word luminous. I explained volume as a shape that rolls out light and inherently controls the way the eye flows as it travels around a three-dimensional form. We started to play and considered a couple of questions.

What happens when a voluminous mass is different in shape than the two basic forms? For example, think of a circle inside a rectangle and triangle. How might we maintain conviction in a work if the internal realms consist of different shapes? I realized that the shapes were like words or thoughts and that a larger vocabulary created more complex and interesting forms. We talked about how a form that was a combination of a rectangle and an oval could be enhanced if we used triangles in the interior. The triangles lent an air of action and hope to the evolution of the oval and the safety of the rectangle.

We talked about symmetry and how it could be a visual distraction. Symmetry was a crutch, used to create balance and a sense of completion in a work that wasn't necessarily finished. We talked about the importance of repetition in shape and in planes. Repetitive shapes enhanced the emotional symbolism of the basic or secondary shape, while graduated planes conveyed a sense of movement, like a series of steps that lead somewhere. The closer together the graduated planes were placed, the more intense the movement in a sculpture became. We talked about the use of a third and fourth shape in the interior of a work. A sculpture with the primary shape of an oval and the secondary shape of a rectangle could be more fully developed by exaggerating the shape of a triangle because the triangle lent a positive note to the symbolism of these shapes. Predictably, as part of the learning process, the blocks came and nobody wanted to work anymore.

My father had a writer's block that lasted for years. He lied about it and told the newspapers that his book was in the editing room of a big publishing house. Instead of confronting his block, he ran away from it. His typewriter gathered dust in the small, cold office adjacent to his bedroom because he couldn't – or wouldn't – write. He slept all day and raged at night. His piano playing came in fits and starts, which for hours disrupted the atmosphere of our home while he tried to play a song he didn't know. He said that jazz was about ear, heart, and soul. It was not about learning to imitate the cry of someone else's experience, so he would not read music. He rejected his failure as an artist by celebrating his success in the world – throwing parties, giving away dinner and drinks at his bar, and volunteering to teach debate at my school. My father determined what we needed and then he made it happen. He did not tell me to be the best at what I do. Instead, he told me to be the best at everything – from how to score a goal, write a poem, read a book, or look at the sky. But he also taught me that the best was never good enough. He never told me what the best was.

I had, of course, encountered my own blocks. I called them my stages of revulsion. When I first started working with sculpture, I couldn't get beyond them. Each time I experienced a block I abandoned the piece, put it on a shelf, and started a new one. Then, as the pieces got more complex, I learned how to work through the first, second, and up to the eleventh stages of revulsion until I worked a piece to death and then some. "Killing" a piece is sometimes the only way to make it come to life. I had to work through whatever idea I was struggling with until it took on a form and life of its own.

I was searching for something – an answer to a particular question, if not a new way of living with my life. I didn't want to spend years running from whatever it was that I ran away from when I was blocked. I didn't have the luxury – or desire – to drink myself into oblivion and step out of my life with different parties or sexual partners. I had children I loved. I didn't want them to grow up knowing that mommy was a coward. I didn't want them to be afraid of pursuing the absolute best because I was afraid of it. I was driven to get beyond my block and to the other side.

I brought two sculptures into my class – my first pregnant woman and a piece not yet finished. I talked to my students about mental blocks and how they occur when we are no longer in control of a piece. I explained that blocks are actually crossroads where what we know and what we want to know converge. I told them that stages of revulsion are part of the process and that each one is a moment to be celebrated.

We stepped back from the work and looked at the geo-metric forms that were happening naturally. We worked at strengthening those forms by executing them with con-viction, by ensuring that the edges were crisp, and convex planes were fluid and uninterrupted. Then we listened to what the pieces were trying to tell us and forgot about what we wanted them to say.

I had the class sculpt for another month. Then, I taught them how to make a waste mold. The process took longer than I had anticipated, and after two nights that lasted until two in the morning, we attempted to open the molds. To our dismay, the plaster was bad and everyone lost every-thing – the molds and the sculptures. I cried before they did. We tried to mend things with plaster and Elmer's glue. We salvaged one piece, threw away the rest, and took com-fort in the process.

Lesson 5

Every sculptural form consists of two basic geometric shapes that interact with each other. The way these two shapes come together and converse determines the experiential expression. The shapes need to be equal in the work – one cannot be dominant over the other – and they need to be clearly defined through volume in the interior of the work. If the work has a dominant shape, the other shape will become inconsequential. Then the work will be either overly sentimental or a static intellectual statement. In other words, it will be boring. It will not reveal self or expand levels of consciousness. Art is not about duplicating an idea or an emotion. It is about the places where ideas and emotion come together.

Musicians understand that great music doesn't happen in the notes or in the chords – not in the melody or in harmony. It happens in the pause between the notes – in the silence. Sculpture is similar. Expression does not come from the triangle or the oval. It occurs at the interstices of planes – that's where the dialogue begins.

CHAPTER 5

Love was the most difficult thing I had ever known. During the first two years of teaching, I often questioned it. I loved my husband, our kids, and our dogs. I loved my work and I loved my students. My entire mindset was about giving to my loves, but I couldn't freeze-frame them, or the constant energy of giving, and take the rest I needed.

I was working on a piece trying to understand love – how to hold it and find solace within it. I couldn't get there. I found only that the connection we strive for when we love – the touching beyond body and into the soul – was impossible for me. I could try to touch and try to know love, but the effort I made only determined the depth of my involvement and the quality of fleeting moments. Love isn't fixed or solid. It requires work – struggle and desire, hope and memory, a momentary pause in intimacy and then the effort to go again, fight again, touch again, and dream again.

I realized why my father never told me what the best meant. He couldn't. The best is never good enough because when you attain it – or you think you attain it – it vanishes only to appear elsewhere, reminding you of the other things you want – another desire, another moment. There is only the reaching and the process.

At that point in my life, I did not love process. I was too busy trying to get somewhere and trying to live two lives – that of an artist and that of a mother and wife. I wanted to push through to an end, a desired outcome. I wanted to sculpt everyday in a light-filled room with flowers and wooden floors. I wanted to hear my children laughing as they played with my husband and at the end of the day see a clean house and happy people. I knew it was idealistic, but the fantasy was my escape. We had moved and my new studio was tiny – an old, one-car garage filled with cobwebs and poor lighting. It leaned slightly to one side and I worried that a strong wind would knock it down.

My children needed me all the time. My husband worked, played computer games, and wanted a wife who would comfort and care for him, bake things, clean house, and at night put a loving head on his shoulder. I was constantly torn between loves. If I gave my energy to my husband and children, then they became the dominant focus and I was lost. If I gave my energy to my art and myself then my family was lost. There was no balance. My life was an either/or situation and I was trying not to choose, trying to bridge the gap with love.

I believed my father had lived two lives. In one, he had a wife, children and a group of regular friends. In the other, he had a mistress, a book, and a nightclub. Twilight was his favorite time of day. He had a cream-colored Oldsmobile with black velour seats that he loved to drive. He would take me driving at twilight through the silent streets of Santa Fe –

down Canyon Road and around the Plaza, up Cerrillos Road and left on St. Mike's, past Hardee's restaurant and the hospital, and down again on Old Santa Fe Trail. We would drive in silence – there was an unspoken code against speaking. We listened to John Coltrane on the eight track player and watched through the car windows as people turned into shadows and lights came on.

I wanted to be in the houses where lights shone warm in the ghostly blue of the night. I wanted to be where there was life and warmth – laughter coming from kids running down the hall, "Star Trek" on TV and the aroma of a cooking dinner wafting from the kitchen. Bath water would be filling the tub, soft and steamy hot. Instead, I sat in the car, my head not high enough to touch the headrest, my body against black velour, inhaling second-hand smoke from the Lucky Strike cigarette burning against my father's fingers.

During these rides, I was a silhouette, a shadow of myself watching my father at the moment when his conflicting worlds disappeared and he could be quiet. I wanted him to talk to me and ruffle my hair so I could speak and be myself. But in that car, when day was turning to night, he was beyond my reach – his thumb tapping on the wheel to a beat I couldn't follow. There was no possibility of the connection I longed for, of the passing of heart into action and mind into words. I wanted to go home, to stop him from disappearing, and to see him display the passion – even if it was directed against me – that made him beautiful. And yet I never spoke during those times and I never turned down the opportunity to ride with him. I thought if I declined his offer, he wouldn't love me anymore. And I thought that if I spoke and broke that silence, he would revoke my privilege to bear witness to his private reveries.

For two years, I listened to Coltrane every night while I worked and tried to understand love. I didn't even like the music. It was melodramatic, raucous, and disturbing, but I listened. I played it as I took my sculpture up and through and down and up again, played it while I tried to understand why my life was split in two. I didn't know I was trying to break beyond the silence of twilight through the violent movement of my fingers working the wax. I didn't know that every time I cut or added, cleaned or mottled, broke a plane or defined one I was playing to the silence of my father driving his car. I had recreated that wall between my father and me in the prison of my marriage and I wanted out. I wanted to hit someone, scream out loud, cry, love and be loved, or at least laugh with someone. I wanted to be home in warm, yellow light. But I could not let go of either of my lives, and I was having difficulty living the twilight time in between.

I thought of crosses, of sacrifice, of the moment when different worlds meet to create a new form from chaos. I loved the idea of the cross, the tension inherent in its form. It framed the collision of two worlds where lives that coexist in union and despair come together or fall apart. What I discovered was that a cross is not a shape. It is a symbol – sometimes of hope, sometimes of power – but is never its own entity. It is only a representation of coexistence. The cross is a dream, a romance or an ideal, an ambition or a desire. The junction between its lines was the determination of my future.

I called my newest piece *Cross to Bear*. It had taken months to complete and I had needed to kill it twice before it took on a form that spoke to me. I had tried to make an actual cross out of figures. In one version, a male figure held a woman across his knees; in another, he held her across his chest. When I finally finished the piece, it didn't look like a cross at all. But there was a cross nonetheless. It was an internal cross, manifested through volume, points of light, and intersecting planes. The piece itself was rectangular with an oval for its secondary form.

Cross to Bear was an excuse for my marriage. Through it, I had the realization that the safety and security inherent in long-term relationships give rise to the need to create separate, yet equal identities. I had sought to recreate through the course of my marriage the mirrors that let me see the picture of myself I had carried since childhood. Without mirrors, I lacked the courage to see myself directly. Instead, I saw a reflection of the persona I had tried to create through the eyes of the man I thought I loved. But somewhere in the process of my marriage, the reflection ceased to be adequate. I got lost in my family, in financial obligations, and cleaning house. My future disappeared. I lost the shape of myself. I was, again, a shadow.

I realized that my mother had been shadow-like as well, sifting slowly across my moments of light. Always in the background – at a soccer game, a sheeted ghost at Halloween, running back and forth between the nightclub and the bookkeeping office – she had been present in my life, but as someone to avoid, to never emulate, to ridicule and fight against. She wore turtlenecks and had short hair. She seldom laughed. She was a small figure, hunched against a noisy life, yet I saw her beauty. Beneath her olive skin, strained pale with exhaustion, there were traces of wealth, sophistication, and confidence.

I never truly knew my mother – except through the accusations of a screaming man desperate to defend his infidelities. "Hey kids, who do you think is brighter, your mother or me?" he asked sarcastically during one of their fights. Sometimes he would look at us while they fought and say, "When was the last time you heard her laugh?" or "Women can't be artists. The only creative thing they'll ever produce is what comes out between their fucking legs." Helplessly, we watched as my mother's lips would tighten, the lines setting more firmly in an already rigid face, confirming to me my father's conviction that she was uptight, and needed to be more for him so he wouldn't have to have a mistress or stay at the club all night and come home drunk and stoned.

One night, my father hit my mother. My sister, brother, and I were home alone sleeping when we heard a crash followed by moaning and crying. My sister and I came out of our room to see what the matter was and saw him dragging my mother into the house by one arm. She was bloody. We wanted to call an ambulance. We wanted to clean her up. I was crying and my sister was yelling – her tears pooling at the corners of her eyes, her face rigid and tight like my mother's.

My father wouldn't let us help her. As he yelled, we backed into our room. He followed us in, slamming the door behind him. He told us not to worry, to stay there and mind our own business, and then he turned to leave. He couldn't open the door. He was too angry to remember that our door had to be pulled to open. So he pushed the door through its frame, splintering the wood. We huddled in our beds terrified of a raging man from whom we only wanted silence and isolated from a broken mother who we thought was dying.

In the morning he was gone. We sponged our mother's face, rubbed toothpaste in her mouth, and eased her into the bathtub hoping she would feel better. "Thank you," she said weakly, "You were right. I do feel better." I loved her then, but only for a moment. I thought *she* was the problem – why my father couldn't write, why he needed to be gone, why he raged and screamed and watched long hours of television naked on his bed. I thought she was his cross to bear.

Until I worked on *Cross to Bear*, I believed that my marriage was not working because I wasn't good enough, because I was too much of a misfit to do anything right. I had given into bankruptcy, broken furniture, and holes in the walls because my husband could not live with a working wife. I once fixed a screen door with leftover parts to save money, but he just laughed at my workmanship and asked me why I even bothered when I knew I couldn't do it right. I stopped trying to fix things. Then he complained they were broken.

Through the years of my marriage, I tried to be all the things I thought my mother was not and still I failed. *Cross to Bear* was an attempt to understand the mystery of marriage and a way to continue to hold it sacred without losing my new-found self-awareness. Because we were each other's crosses to bear, we had the possibility of a shared future. I needed to believe that our discontent was merely the byproduct of our growth. I wanted my marriage to work. I did not know who I was without it.

Over time, I recognized myself outside the circumstance of my marriage. My "no" became as powerful as my husband's, and my "yes" was more often for myself. The cross to bear is that which reveals us to ourselves. Christ could not recognize or accept himself as the Son of God until he carried his cross. We carried our marriage like a cross. Through that process, I had discovered my voice and a method for living. My husband had discovered the Internet. There were nights when we did not speak at all and nights when he tried to reach me by coming into the studio while I worked. I no longer had room for him.

Three years of bruised hands, aching shoulders, and emotional self-examination had moved me further than I cared to explain to him. I felt as though I had launched myself down a mineshaft in a cart I didn't have the ability to steer. Rushing through the dark tunnel, I caught glimpses of things in the air and on the rock walls. I was terrified, yet exhilarated. I felt more alive than I'd ever been in my life. Some nights I would cry as I worked. Burning tears streamed down my face and wax stung my eyes. I cried not out of grief or joy – but because emotionally the art was overpowering. It was too much, too fast as tangled memories and flashing images rushed over me. My languages failed in the moment, leaving me only the tears and the desire to express what I thought I had seen.

The marriage was no longer enough. The junction between lines was the determination of my future, and the junction between my husband and me was well below the center of our cross. I was angry and disgusted with my husband. I had changed but the routines had not. I felt he had never wanted to know me. He only wanted me to live according to his definition of how life was supposed to be. I blamed him for my conflict and didn't want him to touch me. I wanted to know myself as separate and whole, as a unique form that was equally valid, equally strong, and that could not be lost in the shadow of someone else.

I was building a wall between us as I recreated myself. Instead of finding synthesis in my life, I had found that I had to make a choice because I could no longer be who I once was. I had to choose who I wanted to be and how I wanted to live. I started working on a sculpture about being alone.

Lesson 6

*T*here is a significant difference between mass and volume in the sculpting process. Mass is the overall geometric form. Volume has to do with depth inside the form. If we slap on large chunks of clay and smooth them to get a desired shape or speed up the process to arrive at an anticipated outcome, we will eliminate the dynamic of volume in the piece. We need to conceive of each part of the sculpture in depth, and then build each part independently as its own sculptural form. Sculptural expression is the dialogue between these forms – if they do not exist there is nothing to talk about. It is advisable to build with small pieces and press them on rather than smearing them. Smearing can destroy the planes of the shape we are trying to create. It is easier to build each muscle in an arm than it is to build a large mass and then carve the muscle. Carving, in clay, often makes the work look superficial. We need to keep the surface rough. "Smooth" is a texture – part of the finishing process.

CHAPTER 6

In my first three years of sculpting, I realized I had spent a lifetime defining myself using someone else's language. I pursued achievement, tried to make my life a product that fit into a neat package, and mercilessly shut down all the parts of me that didn't fit into it. As I discovered other methods of expression – other languages – I realized I could never fit neatly into any one definition. Every new language gave rise to a multitude of new questions. Sculptural expression, the casting process, body language, and shape theory aroused suspicion that there is more than one truth about any one thing.

I realized that my life was not about a desired outcome or product and I understood that art was not about the completed object. There is no resting place because every completed object is an object only through definition. As definitions evolve through the variety of language, product becomes process. Meaning becomes about asking, not about answers.

The fragmentation of my life seemed to be more about the different languages I used rather than the experiences

I encountered. I became consumed with paradoxes. Why is light both a particle and a wave and why does time exist simultaneously as cyclical and linear? I wanted synthesis in my life, in my languages, and in my understanding of self. Somehow, I had watered down the existentialism I had been fed as a child and my understanding of the philosophy seemed overly self-indulgent and judgmental. I felt there was more, something beyond the crisp-edged planes or soft, sensuous forms where cyclical and linear, particle and wave, idea and emotion came together into something other. It was something I felt, but I did not have the language to express it, let alone explore it further.

My father read Kierkegaard and Camus to us when we were little children and Nietzsche was dinner conversation. But I could never reconcile the concept of Nietzsche's superman – who would build a bridge between society and the individual – with Superman the comic book character. My father taught us about the myth of Sisyphus and reminded us always that Sisyphus was eternally trapped in hell, pushing a giant boulder up a hill. He couldn't escape and he couldn't stop pushing that boulder any more than we could escape our predicaments in life. My father hated Sisyphus and all that Camus had gleaned from the myth, yet he believed in the truth of it. I had believed in it too. But my belief was beginning to waver.

To my knowledge, nobody had ever asked Sisyphus what he thought about pushing the rock up that hill. For all I knew, he might have answered the question with the only definition available to him – "I'm a rock pusher." His answer might be similar to "I'm an iron worker" or "I'm a mother" for that matter. Having no other language and only one process through which to see himself, Sisyphus the rock pusher may have been content. Suddenly, it seemed that truth was a matter of perspective – evolving through the culmination of language and process.

My understanding of myself had grown and I now looked at what it meant to try to live honestly. I was, I felt, living the battle between the idea of free will and the idea of predestination as much as I was wrestling with who I wanted to be and who I was supposed to be. The sculpture I was working on was called *In Time*. It was the largest piece I had ever done and the most painful. I had struggled for years with the deep religious constructs of existentialism and wanted to define individual action as something that was not a reaction to circumstance or to history. I saw free will as an act wrought with the freedom and responsibility of choice. It seemed creative and honest – a step toward God and away from history. Free will was the rejection of predestination and consequently the occurrence of something new. I desperately needed to believe that through an act of pure will, I could transcend myself and begin again.

I understood that momentary catharsis could propel an individual to act independently, without mirrors. And the only way one could step outside of life and see clearly through unbiased eyes would be through tragedy or miracle. I wanted to know what act occurred at the moment of catharsis that propelled an individual out of reaction and into action. I believed self-sacrifice was the key to defining a pure act of will. I had to kill what I knew about myself because that knowledge had been formed without my consent. In that knowledge, I remained predestined, reactive, and condemned to living someone else's idea about who I should be.

As I sculpted this piece about being alone, I examined acts of will that fit my criteria. The first was the frenzied action of a religious fanatic. It seemed to me that when one entered into frenzy one was capable of moving beyond the life one had lived. There was no thought of consequence or remorse for shunning family, job, friends, or home for the love of God. I envied such a frenetic state of mind, but finally concluded that it was the result of some prior experience – mystical or secular – and consequently a reaction. While it appeared that it was an act of self-sacrifice it became, in the end, an act of self-preservation.

The second act I looked at was suicide. I thought about suicide often because my grandfather had committed suicide. My father had told me the story of how his father had ridden the railroad looking for work during the Great Depression and how he ultimately hanged himself in a Florida jail. He spoke of a recurring dream where he dug up his father's bones and smashed them against a tree until he and the bones were bloody, his emotions spent. Through my father's telling, I accepted suicide as an act of courage. Chalmers, my grandfather, was a hero to me. I believed he had the courage to do what my father could not.

I remembered myself at nineteen. At that age, suicide had become more than a romantic idea. I had lived enough by then to believe that the life my father had described did not exist. Early one morning after a night of heavy drinking, I drove my truck into the rear of another kid's car and was arrested. I was drunk and in jail. I had been exposed. That dark thing I had been running from had surfaced – and it was me. With that realization, I could not face being bailed out by the man who would later become my husband and knowing that this man who I wanted to love would see what I knew to be true about myself. I wanted the dark thing dead. I took off my bra, wrapped one strap around the light in the jail cell, and the other strap around my neck.

I did not succeed in killing myself. I was being watched on a video monitor and the cops burst in and took my bra, my shoelaces, and talked about taking my shirt. Then my boyfriend, a cop himself, arrived in full police uniform and bailed me out. I was destroyed. I didn't want him to see me like this or to know this part of me. I tried to jump out of his car on the highway home. He reached across me and held the door. I opened the compartment where he kept his gun and he hit my hand away. As he drove, the night rushed past. I was in tears, yelling, and in self-indulgent desperation. When we got to my house, he grabbed his gun and I ran away, my head reeling from the alcohol I had consumed. I hid under a car while he called for me. I did not want to be found.

At some point, a salmon-streaked morning sky illuminated my surroundings and I found myself in the cab of a truck in the middle of a neighborhood I didn't recognize. I began to knock on doors trying to find my way home, but only one person answered. When he opened the door, his eyes went wide and he quickly slammed it shut. I looked down and saw that I had lost my pants. I was naked from the waist down. My legs were muddy and cut. By the time I found my way home I was sober – straight-faced and hopeless. The last vestige of self-respect had been lost in the wanderings of the night and there was nothing left. My boyfriend hugged me when I came back. Tears formed at the corners of his eyes. We slept awhile, then he packed us a bag and we drove to Maine. He told me that he loved me and, in so doing, gave me a choice. In that moment, it was enough for me to hold on to, enough for me to again relegate the thought of suicide to the back of my mind. At first glance, suicide had appeared to be an act of self-sacrifice, but it was only a reaction to circumstance. The possibility of suicide spoke of awareness without faith. It was the ultimate acceptance of and resignation to a life and an identity not of my creation.

As I worked *In Time*, I was consumed by my past – not only by my immediate experience, but also by the entirety of a past that spanned thousands of years – culturally, historically, and socially. Suddenly, a cloak emerged around the sculpture and it seemed to me that the figure was hidden beneath it, safe from the life experience that assaulted her. She was retreating, losing herself instead of moving into herself. I could not get her to escape the circumstance of her existence. She wore this cloak of collective history and it weighed upon her even while it offered protection against the personal experiences that crawled up and over her in countless shapes and shadows. I did not know how I could escape the force of my culture and its history even if I managed to transcend the effects of my own experience. I looked for synthesis in the form – the coming together of self-awareness with personal and collective experience – because synthesis was the only thing I could conceive of that spoke of something new. I needed the sculpture to show me how to exercise my will through the process of my experience. I could not accept that my pursuit was in vain.

Up to this point, I had been recycling snatches of knowledge I gleaned from conversations beyond my comprehension and from a smattering of books I read. I was trapped in what I thought I knew, trapped in a two-thousand-year-old tradition of thought and process, and trapped in my training and limited education. Philosophical fragments peppered my methods of expression and clouded the questions I was trying to ask. The cloak of history my figure wore appeared like a death shroud and was inescapable. Even if I could free myself from my personal experience, I saw no way out of Western civilization. Maybe I needed to go into my experience – both personal and historical – instead of out of it to find the thing I sought.

I had started *In Time* in water-based clay thinking she was so large I wouldn't be able to model her in wax. Over the course of a few months – during which I questioned suicide and religious fanaticism – the figure had hardened and cracked. I was forced to work the surface and to play with line instead of plane. By the time I realized that I needed to go into my experience – instead of out of it – the piece had been spray-painted, sanded, reinforced with wood, and her cracks patched with wax.

I was still working at the foundry at this time, making molds, chasing metal and doing patinas. I had learned that the word *sincere* originated from an Italian foundry term meaning without wax. Foundries use wax to patch casting flaws in areas that cannot be welded. A sincere bronze is one that has no wax in it. It is pure. I thought about being sincere. I wanted to work more than the surface of my sculpture and I wanted to access more than the surface of myself. I molded the sculpture and cast her in solid wax so that she was of one medium, pure. Then I started cutting.

Lesson 7

Rebuilding a sculpture after you have carved too much away can be a difficult process. As you begin, try to remember the original points of reference you identified at the onset. They provided opportunities to create parallels for the external geometric shapes in the interior of the piece and helped you to develop the dialog in the sculpture. Finding them again and articulating volume around them will help you identify your initial intent and recreate flow.

CHAPTER 7

Artistic creation became a pathway for me and I thought it could be the act of will I desired. Through it, I began a process of examining my experience and questioning my truths. The languages I learned had made me more aware, and trained my mind to consider things from different perspectives. The pursuit of art gave me breath and, in turn, life. But it also took me away from my family and the life I once knew into a solitude that had brutal consequences.

A deluge of small and large catastrophes dominated my domestic life and I felt increasingly hopeless. I spent days hunting for a treasured stuffed animal that had been lost somewhere in the yard and didn't find it. I had been forbidden to hold a regular job and we perpetually faced financial disaster. My husband drank more, raged more frequently, and worked fewer hours. Neighbors complained about our dogs and animal control officers were always on our doorstep. I could not keep the dogs in the yard any more than I could stop what was happening in my home.

In spite of it all, I kept working. My studio was a safe place and artistic process was like magic. I would start off with a block of wax or clay then shape, model, and carve it, building up and out until a form appeared – the rough outlines of a vision or a dream. From chaos came order, from aspiration came answers. Through sculpture, hope materialized as something concrete and touchable. It existed in the world as a solid object and had a shadow of its own. Sometimes I felt that someone or something was channeling my hands and eyes to say something I was incapable of knowing or expressing on my own. I had to sculpt because for me, not sculpting was somehow a rejection of God.

Artistic creation seemed to fit all my criteria for an act of will – from self-awareness to self-sacrifice. But as I worked this sculpture and lived my life, I realized that the pursuit of art – in and of itself – was not enough to transcend myself. Through art I had the opportunity to examine my experience, to see it in a new light, to shift my perceptions, and, consequently, my truths. Art helped me to process what I had seen and known, but it failed as an act of will because it could not exist independently outside of my history. Artistic process was a reaction to my life through which I found ways to accept and live with myself. It did not give me the means to suspend my past and begin anew. It remained, simply, a record of my questions, the documentation of my experience, and the expression of my faith.

I felt I was spiraling. I had started small, like a tight circle moving up and out of my knowledge and method of interpretation. Through language and process, the circles had widened. I became more aware. I occupied more space. The sculpture took more time. I drew spirals on scraps of paper and rearranged the planes on my figure so that the points of light moved spiral-like. As the spirals moved through experience – up and around the sculpture – they widened. I knew that at some point the spiral would leave the figure and travel out and away, continuing on and ever expanding through unmapped territory. I believed that as the spiral opened it would transcend the figure. The marks of her experience would remain, but they would be far below and of little consequence. If she could keep spiraling up and away from the center, then she would ultimately leave her experience and understanding of self behind. She would have to recreate herself as the spiral traveled because the mass that had been her identity could not travel with her. Her spirit could move. Her body could not. She was closer to the moment of transition when she would have to choose between leaving her body forever or continuing to recreate the pattern of her experience.

Trees are spirals. I would lie on the ground as my children played at the park and look through the branches to the sky. The branches grew in a spiral pattern that traveled up and out from the center of the trunk – like fingers reaching toward eternity. But they never got there, they only reached. Finally, it appeared to me that the only way the tree could live was to systematically recreate itself in the same pattern and from the same material.

It was exactly that pattern of re-creation from which I was trying to escape. I did not want to replicate my experiences, spiraling on and on to a moment when my spirit left my body and my only choice was to die.

I thought I had been too self-absorbed and/or too intellectual. Trapped in my mind and body, and separated with intent from the everyday occurrences that had made life rich for me, I considered the last act that might be an act of will. I knew that will had to involve self-sacrifice and cathar-sis had to come from some kind of death, be that physical, metaphysical, or spiritual. I had considered sacrificing for God, physical self-sacrifice, and sacrifice for art. I had not looked at sacrifice for humanity. I had not considered an act of kindness. I did not know what a true act of kindness was.

I thought about my life and the gifts I had tried to give. Each day felt like a sacrifice because in my mind the needs of my kids and husband always came first. There were the interruptions in the middle of the night. Bad dreams, wet beds, or hunger dragged me from sleep and I had to be kind and soft as I comforted my children. My husband's needs made me sacrifice the person I wanted to be. I believed I was responsible for both the physical and emotional well-being of everyone in my family and that meant that my well-being was much less a priority.

A few years prior, during the Christmas season, my husband wished out loud for the electric train set he never got as a child. But he thought our children were still too young to have anything like that in the house. He couldn't wait for them to get older so he would have an excuse to buy it. I thought I could give him his wish.

After he went to work the next day, I went to the lumberyard and purchased the wood to build him a train table. I hid the wood in our neighbor's shed and worked every day during the kids' naptime until the table was done. It was six feet long by eight feet wide and stood four feet off the ground.

Then I bought the train set. There were enough tracks to fill the table, an assortment of miniature trees and signs, and a *Santa Fe Railroad* engine with several cars. I bought fake grass and foam rubber so my husband could make the hills and valleys through which the train would travel. On the night before Christmas, I dragged the train table into the room I used as a studio. It took up half of my workspace, but that didn't matter. Finally, I wrapped each car, section of track, and accessory separately and put them on the table. Then I wrapped the table itself and turned out all the lights.

He came home late that night and did not see his gift. When morning came, we went downstairs with the kids to open presents and I watched his face. He grinned at the immensity of his wrapped gift and looked at me curiously with a raised eyebrow. I wouldn't let him open it right away. First, we let the kids open their gifts. Then he gave me a jacket. Finally, it was his turn. He ripped off the paper on the table and his forehead furrowed. He couldn't figure out why I had built this huge table. Then he started to open the train set. When he turned to hug me, I was startled. He didn't look happy. He looked like you do when you receive a very expensive gift that wasn't what you had in mind.

I tried to ignore the look on his face and started to help him open the rest of the set. He suggested we have coffee and then clean up some of the mess. Later in the day, I reminded him that he hadn't finished un-wrapping his gifts. He said he would rather wait until after the kids were in bed so he could concentrate fully on setting things up. But that night, he drank too much wine and became tired. He said he would get back to the train set in the morning.

Eventually, he did build the hills and valleys and set up the track. The train ran a few times and then it sat there, taking up half my studio space and gathering dust. In the early part of summer, I asked him if he was ever going to use it. "Probably not," he said. So we took the train set apart and put it in boxes. Then we dismantled the table and turned it into a playhouse for the kids.

I had wanted to give my husband a gift that spoke to who I thought he was. I wanted him to know that he could be who he wanted to be and that he was loved. A store-bought gift – a new razor or a nice piece of clothing – didn't mean very much to me. The train set was a gift of love because it demonstrated my willingness to share my studio space and it encouraged him to be himself. But the gift killed his fantasy. I had taken away his ability to choose or create the thing himself. I thought I had demonstrated an act of kindness. Instead, I took his independence. An act of kindness was not an act of will. An act of will was supposed to make me feel bigger and better instead of small and wrong.

I had taught my students that an artistic block was a gift – an opportunity to go beyond what you knew. It was a crossroad where what you thought you knew and what was revealed through your work met, determining the future of the piece and the future questions you would become capable of asking. Blocks were to be celebrated because on the other side was truth. But I had never encountered a block this serious before. All the things I had considered as an act of will had failed my criteria and I was stuck.

I knew I was missing a piece. There had to be a connection between action and experience, between free will and predestination because they seemed to exist simultaneously in time and space. I was straddled between art and family and I knew one fed the other. I could not create art without living in the world and I could not live in the world without creating art. I needed to be a mother and a wife. I also needed to be a sculptor.

The paradoxical life I was living was tearing me apart. It didn't make rational sense. Light is both particle and wave. Time is measured as both cyclical and linear. We name things and people, define them in singular terms and expect that our definitions will stop change and reveal the mysterious essence of whatever enigma presented itself for definition. But definitions are, at best, descriptors. They reveal only one possibility of understanding or a paradox that leaves one unsure of the meaning or identity of that enigma. I am a woman. I am a mother. I am a wife. I'm someone's daughter. I am a sister. I am a friend to many. I am a teacher and a student. And I am an artist. I have many titles, but no clear definition of who I am. I also know that I could not exist as myself without fulfilling each of the roles in which I choose to function. I was doing a sculpture about being alone and learning that I could never be alone. My life was my choice and my frustration with it was the product of my self-victimization.

I was not content because I chose not to be. I dwelled on my past and saw only pain. I looked at my marriage and saw only what didn't work. I looked at myself and saw only what I didn't like. I chose reaction as the tool that allowed me to measure my growth. I defined myself through the rejection of myself because that was the process I understood as self-examination.

When my father told me of Sisyphus and angst, he convinced me that through self-examination, Sisyphus would have realized continuing to push the boulder up the hill – and having it forever rolling down again – was absurd. Through Sisyphus, my father taught me that it was my responsibility as an intelligent individual to examine myself, to shed layer after layer of beliefs until I came to the inevitable truth that I, myself, am absurd – pointless and without a purpose. Only then would I become capable of embracing existential angst and be fully alive.

I realized my pursuit of what I still understood to be his truth had driven me to reject every facet of my life. Even after his death, I still wanted my father to approve of me; I wanted to encounter angst and, consequently, myself as nothing so he would love me. Through that process, I had become incapable of loving myself.

I had instructed my students to be open to their work and embrace the fact that they couldn't know how a piece was going to turn out because sculpture was a process of questions, of trial and error, and, in the end, revelation. I told them that if I knew what I wanted in a piece, I would build a table, not create a sculpture. The process of self-examination is about asking questions, not getting to a pre-determined answer. My life and art coexisted because art was the language through which I could question my life.

I understood *In Time*. It revealed that while I could never suspend my past and be born again, I could forgive it and cease its effects on me. Through forgiveness, experience would become something that moved through me, something that did not need reaction. Instead of being solid – rock-like and hard – I could become more fluid, like water. I could move and shift, allowing things to pass through me without losing my fundamental identity. Ultimately, I realized that transcending me was rhetoric, and what I really wanted to do was to put the past to rest so I could live with myself.

But I did not know how to forgive. I did not know how I would live without fighting. As long as I had something to measure myself against, I had the motivation to overcome obstacles, to look for alternative solutions, and to question and probe. I did not believe I could exist without that measure, without reacting to someone or something. My past was the tool I had used to build my life. If I forgave it – became like water and let experience move through me – I would stop becoming. I would have to just be. I had found my act of will, but I was incapable of performing it. I thought I would never sculpt again. I thought I had gone as far as I could go. I could envision my future, but I could not fully realize it. I could not act because I could not forgive. Then my marriage dissolved and my world shattered. The jarring reality of my present shouted down my past. For the second time in my life, I existed without form.

Lesson 8

We tend to look at the light when we look at a sculpture. Light reflects off the high points and creates flow. We follow light around the piece. We recognize the shapes each point of light helps to create and we react to them. They empower us. We seldom look at the shadows because shadows can be frightening. Yet shadows are often more important than light. Not only do shadows occur at the intersection of planes and the moment of expression, they reveal to us the possibility of mystery. They make us want to go inside, to look again at what is being said, and go deeper into the work and into ourselves. We have all experienced those places inside of us that reject definition, that do not cooperate with words. Those are powerful places. Shadow areas are similar. In sculpture, a tangible triangle is not about the triangle. It is about our objective interaction with it. On the other hand, a triangle that is recessed or made through negative space is about the triangle. In spite of the fact that a triangle inspires a desire to climb upward, we cannot engage with the illusion of a triangle, we can only contemplate it. Shadows speak paradoxes and reveal other truths.

CHAPTER 8

I came home. I brought with me an armful of children, a washer and dryer, ten boxes of books, tools, clothes, toys, my work tables, and an old, black trunk full of failed casting that spoke courage to me across two thousand miles and onto the deck of my childhood.

My mother's house was a large A-frame with gable windows like an upside down jack-o-lantern. Inside, the walls were lined with thousands of books and pictures angled to the pitch of the roof so that they stared down at you. There was the grand piano that nobody played anymore and it fought with a Nordic track for space in the crowded living room.

It still felt cold in spite of a new roof and insulation. Though it was summer, there was snow on the mountains and not much light in the house. There was wood to be chopped, plumbing that needed fixing, a bathroom in need of new tiles, and horses to be tended. There were miles of forests and few people. There was my mother, older now and beautiful again. She was smiling. She filled the house

with food and made the beds. She found old, stuffed animals, and decorated the kids' room with them. She had
time again to listen, talk, and read. There was the stream
behind the house and gooseberry bushes. There was the
large blue spruce I'd climbed as a child that now drapes
and protects my father's grave.

The grave isn't really a grave. It is a marker over buried
ashes. I always wanted it to be a grave. I wanted there to be
bones under that tree. Ashes don't mean anything. They
are the waste, not the essence of the person. On the marker
is his epitaph. He wrote it the morning he died: "I am the
night descending, the breath of God. I am timeless now, or
rather, I am time itself." It had always surprised me that he
knew he was going to die and I had always wanted to know
what he meant by "the breath of God." I thought that life
was about breath, not dying.

I took over the deck, which became a makeshift studio.
Through the summer – while my children discovered a
world without fences or television – I sat there in the sun
sculpting every random idea that floated into my head. I
was a dandelion puff drifting high in the air. There was
nothing to anchor me to the ground, nothing to determine
my course. I rose with the wind, spinning randomly, lazily,
with no destination and no desire.

Truth was a matter of perception and my perception was
flawed. My marriage had been a lie, and I was home again
with nowhere to go and no reason for going. My husband
had told me stories about himself, about what he believed
and what he desired. I had believed in his stories but he
had lied. His stories were fiction, and I was merely a fig-
ment of his imagination, a character created from the raw
material of me at nineteen.

For eleven years, I believed in him and thought I was the problem. For eleven years, I told myself that if I could only change, things would get better and he would touch me as though he loved me and would listen like he cared. But he was not real, and I was not real in relationship to him. Through the course of our marriage, his lies had been slowly killing me because I did not know they were lies.

During that summer, I talked with my mother and re-tiled her bathroom. I taught my kids how to catch a snake and ride a horse. I watched the days roll toward autumn and dreaded having to live in the world again. I didn't trust myself. All my life, I had the luxury of asking why. Why do I live? Why do I love? Why do you love me? Why do we fight? Asking why allowed me to look at the points of light that made my life flow. This question was an easy thing, a diversion. It was a lovely game of cause and effect that began with assumptions that never got anywhere or changed anything. The question, "Why?" permitted me the luxury of rarely having to deal with my day-to-day life. Now, in reaction to the end of my marriage, I had to look at the shadows. I had to ask, "How? How do I live, how do I love, how do I fight?" My mother never had to ask why, she just knew.

When I first lived in this house, I wore patent leather shoes and fancy dresses. I remember the house having no insulation and no gables and we did not have a telephone. We were isolated. The house was ten miles from the nearest year-round neighbor and completely surrounded by National Forest. Often the car got stuck and we would have to walk miles up the un-graded dirt road to get home. Sometimes we got trapped in the canyon by the deep snows or because a car wouldn't start. Then, if there wasn't food in the house, we foraged for canned goods in neighboring cabins. The pipes often froze and there would be no water. The electricity would go out in high winds. But we persevered. My father read books – sometimes two or three a day – and my mother taught school. We ate macaroni and cheese or fried bologna on the stairs for lack of a table.

Not until I was an adult did I learn that my mother had, at that time, taught school in Taos, a town more than three hours away. I did not know that she walked to the end of our canyon, then hitchhiked into Santa Fe and then, again, to Taos. She would leave the house at four in the morning to be at school by eight. Coming home, she walked the road in the dark, sometimes with groceries, arriving in time to cook dinner, bathe us and put us to bed. The remainders of her evenings were spent listening to my father talk about what he had read and written. I never understood why she made those choices. She said that art was the foundation of her marriage, and its center. She said he taught her how to think and how to learn and that was worth everything. But, she added, he wasn't about to do the cooking.

How my mother chose to live was more important than why and that made life possible for the rest of us. In the years before the nightclub, her teaching allowed my father to write. It put food on the table and ensured we had warm clothes, heat, and a safe bed to sleep in at night.

The question, "How?" is about faith. It assumes that the question, "Why?" has been answered by something bigger than yourself. For my mother, "Why?" was answered by her belief that art spoke truth, that it revealed sacred mysteries and offered both explanation and salvation. How she chose to live was her ritual of worship and prayer. My question, "Why?" had been answered first by my father, and after his death, by my marriage, husband and kids.

On the sun-bathed deck, with wax in my hands and my children laughing, I understood relationships must be about how you live, and never why, because you can only have faith in something larger than yourself. At that moment, I had neither the how nor why of my life. Still, it was expected that I act. My only choice was to move out and move on. Questioning memories was getting in the way of living, and choosing how to live seemed like the best way to discover why to live. So I took a part-time job and a falling-down apartment, registered my children for school, and in the process, I met someone new.

Lesson 9

*E*very form in a sculpture has an associated symbolic meaning. Each shape is representative of a particular moment that led to the emotional and intellectual experience we are trying to express. Here's a simple example. Imagine that it is evening and I am cooking dinner while my children play. They are racing remote control cars across the floor. The telephone rings and it is a bill collector. The telephone does not quite reach the stove and dinner is starting to burn. A remote control car overturns the dog's water bowl and I can smell the chicken burning. I hang up the phone, turn to the stove, and a remote control car smashes into my shin. I explode.

As I sculpt this moment of total frustration and irritation, I must include a representation of each of the events leading up to it. The inverted triangle in the cheekbone might be the telephone ringing. It is repeated with force, in the sharp angle of the rib, which indicates the overturned water bowl. The square of the jaw, the shoulders and the stomach might be representative of feeling trapped or powerless. I must try to represent all relevant experience to honestly describe and express that moment. I have to flesh out my shapes, and develop them like characters in a book. If I do not, the emotion remains static and unconvincing. Abstract concepts can be defined only through concrete experience.

CHAPTER 9

Rage consumed me like a virus. A sneeze, at first hardly noticeable, got bigger and more intense until it became a cough deep in my chest that tore at my lungs, spewed bile into my mouth, and interfered with my sleep at night. Like at my father's grave – and with the cigarettes I smoked incessantly – I had believed that smoke was essence and ashes were waste and I was the catalyst through which the metamorphosis of cigarette to smoke and ashes could occur. I wanted to breathe unimpeded, without the smoke or the ashes, but I did not know where to find my essence without them.

My children and I lived in a home that was old, broken down and far too big for us. The roof had been leaking for years and parts of the floor had dry rot. The water came through old, iron pipes and smelled of sulfur. There were three enormous fireplaces. The kids could stand in them and for the first time, there was no question about how Santa Claus would fit through the chimney. The ceilings were ornate and the moldings were hand-carved.

The heater didn't work and the children, wrapped in blankets, huddled close to the fire and got ashes on their toes. We danced to the music of Janice Joplin, Ella Fitzgerald, Ray Charles, and Counting Crows. In the evenings after dinner, my sleepy children leaned softly against each other on the couch, listening in silence as I read to them. And each evening, they tried to stay awake so the story would go on and they would not have to crawl into cold beds where mice droppings often fell through the latillo ceilings above them.

I was pregnant. At first, I thought it was the stomach flu and ignored it, hoping it would go away. It did not. Geoff, the man I was dating, had never experienced the possibility of fatherhood. He was jubilant. He thought I would keep the baby and we would live together, raising his child and making art like some far-out, early seventies song. He was wrong. I would not have another child. I could barely support the children I already had. I would have to work all the time or not work at all. I would be condemned to living with mice and dripping ceilings for too long. I would not have another child and be bound by circumstance to a man for whom I had no love.

For the first time in many years, I was free to make my own decisions. I had ideas and possibilities for a different kind of life. I was going to live without conflict. I was not going to straddle myself between art and family anymore. Instead, I would live according to the dictates of my dreams. I could not be pregnant again with someone else's desire for me to be only what he needed.

When I worked at the foundry, a piece came in that we nicknamed THE CREEPING JESUS. It was made by an amateur sculptor who wanted to preserve it for posterity but didn't want to spend the money on either bronze or a rubber mold. He insisted that a plaster cast be made from a waste-mold. Rick told him he would lose detail in the work. The mold maker explained that hydra-cal, the casting plaster, was not easy to rework. The man did not care. He knew what he wanted. So the waste-mold was made, as was the plaster cast, and the man came into the foundry to view his work.

His sculpture had become hard, white and unforgiving. There were air bubbles, parting line marks, and garish flaws in the anatomy. The piece the man had held in his heart was gone. The sculpture was no longer malleable, no longer the color of the earth, and no longer the product of his care. The man finally saw that his sculpture was not a complete work. The body was merely a mass – a rough form with scratches for a beard, lumps for hair, and bones that looked like they were made from rubber bands. The hands and feet were more carefully worked. Unfortunately, they had been worked so painstakingly that they had nothing to do with each other or with the sculpture as a whole. THE CREEPING JESUS was a body shape with hands and feet that looked like they were from four different people attached to it.

The man had lost control of his creation. He saw only what he was willing to see and because of that he was not prepared to deal with the consequences of his actions or the truth they revealed. He was in a moment of catharsis. He had never worked plaster and the casting plaster we used was especially hard to manipulate. He did not have the skills to fix the mistakes he had made. To work the piece in its new form, he would have to acquire new tools, learn a new language, and begin a new process. He did not make that choice. It was easier for him to blame the foundry for destroying his art and it was easier for him to remake the same sculpture in clay.

I was like the artist who created THE CREEPING JESUS. I wanted the process of becoming to stop. I wanted to know what happened at the end. I wanted a place of rest and not this perpetual struggle. I spent years sculpting the hands and feet of my life because in them I had recognized a small, manageable portion of the thing in which I believed. Marriage and children, as well as teaching and art, were the appendages that created movement and I had worked them feverishly. When my work was cast, however, my lack of attention to the greater whole was blatantly evident and I had neither the language nor the tools to begin a new process with grace. I had always pursued something untouchable, something that shifted and changed, and that I believed was outside of myself. Like smoke and ashes, this thing had an odor and many shapes, but I could not hold it and I could not see it because it was inside me. It was my breath.

So, under a cloud of Valium, green plants and water-color landscapes, I lay upon a table and let them scrape and suck the child out of me to the rhythm of Dvořák. Geoff sulked, believing he had lost his last chance to be a father. I chastised him for his selfishness and celebrated my power of choice. Maybe I had misunderstood my father's teaching; maybe the blood between my legs did demonstrate the creative thing I was capable of producing. My responsibility did not necessarily imply acceptance and my fate could be altered, if not determined, by a word. I told Geoff to leave. I changed my pads and took antibiotics. I threw away my only Dvořák tape and moved my work tables out of the cold and into the living room.

At that moment, I realized that this was my life – right now, not tomorrow, and not yesterday. I understood the possibility that the present occurs only when I rise up to meet whatever is coming down. The present is an act of courage. It is an hourglass where the triangle of hope and inspiration meet, with equal force, the inverted triangle of fear and danger. At that intersection, I occupy the negative space and am bigger than either shape. I am the form, and my power is centered where faith and fate converge. With this knowledge, I believed, again, in process.

We start with an idea or a belief in something larger than ourselves. Like a dog stretching his neck toward a gift of food from a stranger, we reach for that thing in which we believe. The object of our belief lives in shadow. We cannot see it. As we move toward it, we touch others reaching for the same thing, and a connection is made between us – a momentary pause through intimacy. At this intersection, the connection between us reveals the elusive thing we both seek. Our junction creates a possibility of something bigger than either of us and different; the object of our shared faith is visible. But due to the fact that we have seen and touched it, it ceases to be an object of faith. It is then only a method for our connection.

Inside the self or outside the self the process is the same. Concrete experience meets concrete experience and creates abstract truth. Abstract truth becomes concrete experience and the process begins again. We believe in something larger than ourselves and then we create it. Once we have created it, we become it. We imagine, we seek, we create, and we become. I was at the moment of intersection. I was in the present. I had become.

Lesson 10

Sculpture must never be a statement – it can only be a series of questions. Art is the process of self-examination. We need to ask the following questions: What is my subject? Who am I in relation to it? How do my definitions of my subject relate to or determine who I am?

A former student of mine attempted to sculpt a pregnant woman. She thought that a pregnant woman was supposed to be beautiful, feminine, soft, radiant and powerful. As she worked her piece, she became increasingly frustrated. All the power in her piece got lost when she tried to soften her form and emphasize the roundness of pregnancy. In time, she realized that her own experience with pregnancy had been anything but radiant, nurturing and powerful. She had hated being pregnant. She was tired all the time, her back hurt, and she lost her mobility and freedom. She was afraid of the responsibility of motherhood. Unconsciously, she was trying to sculpt someone else's idea of pregnancy and not her own, the reality of which was not what it was supposed to have been. When she understood her own definition of pregnancy and who she was in relationship to that definition, she began to understand how she could live with herself outside the definitions society had imposed upon her. Then her sculpture became a work about the conflict within herself, rather than an idea about pregnancy and it started to speak.

CHAPTER 10

Living in the present meant that I had to stop reacting to what I wanted to see and acknowledge that there was more to the story of life and death than what had been convenient for me. I had to allow other perspectives of my experience into my consciousness and grant them equal weight.

My father died on June 20, 1981 – the day before Father's Day and two days before my sister's sixteenth birthday. We were going on a camping trip. We were going to learn how to wind surf. For just a few days, we were going to be a family whose actions recognized and demonstrated the bonds of love in a conventional way. En route to the campsite, my father stopped for wine and ice cream. We became giddy with sugar and sang several songs. I remember the car stank from the panting of the dogs and too much cigarette smoke, stale in the heat of the sun. The slow, silk burn of the wine had wound its way through the blood of my parents and they were easy in their smiles, quick in the glances they exchanged with each other, and quiet in their

remonstrations against the three children poking each
other with sticky fingers in the back seat.

I never saw it coming. I turned at the last instant as my
mother screamed, "Mike!" and my father swore a long, loud,
"God, Noooooo!" We didn't even have time to put our hands
up in self defense before the other car was on top of us. And
then my father was dead. The scattered frenzy of emergency
workers, the crying and moaning of my siblings, the shout-
ing of bystanders and the wail of sirens, served as a backdrop
for the fly that buzzed around my head as I lay under a blanket in the sun. I needed to see my father. I will forever wish
I had resisted that impulse. Ignoring my mother's screams
to lie down, I threw off the blanket and ran to the bent and
broken car. Suddenly, my whole understanding of the world
was shattered. My father was, in death, just dead. Yellow bile
dripped from his mouth. His eyes were open but vacant. His
body slumped. The scent of Old Spice mingled with fear
and feces. He could have been any man. In that moment,
when I witnessed the absence of light in this man I loved, my
father became merely human and forever silent. His words
and actions had defined me and my world. Without him, I
believed I also ceased to exist. I could not cry at his service.

Like my father's death, the abortion caused me to shut
down my emotions and live in an abstract mind. I shifted
my experience into concepts and ideas fairly remote from
actual occurrences. I thought I could see the big picture
and stay ahead of it, perhaps even control it. But I never
did. I kept moving and changing, growing and reaching.
Life moved of its own accord. The harder I tried to create
my future, the more frustrated I became. It was time to let
life be what it was, time to let me be part of life instead of a
witness to it. It was time for *now*.

The metamorphosis of concrete experience to abstract ideas had been valuable in understanding my questioning process. Yet I felt I could not get beyond the patterns in my life and in my art unless I looked at both from a different perspective. I began to work in the abstract, trying to transform ideas into concrete expression.

I had taught my students that each shape has an individual identity and symbolic association – that sculpture can only exist as an art form when two or more shapes interact with each other and with intent. Every time one shape leaps up and says, "Look at me, I exist!" it presents an opportunity to examine that existence and reframe the definition of the whole. It does not become the whole.

The meaning of the story of Sisyphus and his rock can be defined from a variety of perspectives. From my perspective, he might look like a square and I might define myself as a triangle. But that definition is only my perspective and can occur only in relationship to me and my current definition of self. The object of art is not merely to state my awareness of a particular perspective. It is to try to understand why I chose that perspective and to reveal, through a process of questioning, other simultaneous perspectives which are then represented within the context of the whole.

I believed my shape theory would communicate human experience and could provide, through abstraction, the perspectives I desired. I wanted to talk about the coalition of self. I wanted to see myself as proactive instead of reactive and I wanted to explore the possibility that the internal process of definition had the power to determine external events.

Until this time, I had little interest in abstract art. Most of what I had seen was cold and institutional. Contemporary abstract works reminded me of machines, of the industrial world, of things not human. Occasionally, abstract work suggested something more anthropomorphic. Broad, smooth planes and sensuous curves implied the rise of a breast or what a woman might look like from inside. But often this kind of work moved into the realm of sentiment by winding ribbons of bronze through the air in little wisps and curls that ignored the impact of negative space and shadow. Other works abandoned the aesthetic altogether. Different artists flung skulls haphazardly across piles of rocks, mounted mouth retainers to football trophies, and bound mannequins with barbed wire and broken glass. At worst, modern abstract art seemed to be a scream of impotence and rage; at best, it was a statement of hopelessness and frustration. I had stayed away from it with intent. Now it excited me.

Abstract art could be anything as long as the rules inherent in the language of sculpture – the language of shape – were observed. In any sculpture, a statement of personal experience cannot be an assumption of universal truth. And while it is important for us to recognize that on occasion we can all feel trapped, frustrated, angry, sad or victimized, it is equally important to recognize that in so many ways these experiences are entirely personal.

The expression of individual action and experience is relevant only to the individual unless it is communicated in a way that reveals a larger construct or provides a richer vocabulary. Through this vocabulary, we can process our own experience and exercise our will. A scream of rage and impotence or a statement of frustration and hopelessness are irrelevant when they are used as mass generalizations of social discontent. Art has to go further. It has to recognize the circumstance of experience – one's history – and the reaction of the individual to that circumstance. Then it has to express why the individual reacted in that particular way and, through a process of dialog between forms, present another perspective that enhances viewer awareness and provides opportunity for greater understanding.

In a barn raising, people come together and erects a structure that will become a vital part of their community. While working together, there is cooperation, frustration, sometimes injury, and always celebration. It can be a joyous event that has the power to enrich the lives of those who participate, but to paint a picture of the event and only express the joyous experience would be merely a documentation of history from one person's perspective. To create an artistic expression of the event, a variety of human emotions and experiences must be related. Perhaps there is a small child sitting under a tree and crying because he has hurt his thumb. Perhaps there is a neighbor who could not afford the materials to build his barn that year, and in his face we see envy or resignation. Maybe the wife of the farmer with the new barn conveys a look of relief because her husband will come to bed at night with fewer worries and there will be more money for other necessities. Each individual experience during the event is relevant to a larger understanding of community and us within it. It is not enough for me just to say, "I am happy!" in my painting. I must demonstrate the complexity of human experience from which that emotion arises so that the work can generate a larger understanding of my own, as well as other's, experiences.

The abstract sculpture I was working on was called *Now*. It illuminated the fact that my life had consisted of a series of relationships where the expression of one individual was dominant over the other and, as such, my life was a static statement of intellect or sentiment. These relationships defined who I was because my interaction was always reactive. Sometimes I had control and my desires, needs, and wants determined the course of events and the actions of others. Sometimes I relinquished it. Then, I swayed like flotsam on a pond, my direction determined by each new wave or ripple that occurred. I liked it better when I was in the dominant position, when I was the wave instead of the flotsam, but neither position was satisfactory. In both situations, I was in constant reaction to people and circumstances outside of myself. Every choice I made was in direct response to the actions of those with whom I was involved.

The abstract method of expression was allowing me to see other perspectives within the construct of a single form. It revealed the possibility of a larger understanding by demonstrating that individual experience is almost always dictated by what has occurred previously and by our desire to either stop that feeling from recurring or to ensure that it does. Individuals move through the present and their actions create it, but they cannot express it because their perspective is bound by a trajectory from past to future.

Abstract expression freed me from the figurative trap of an individual in reaction to her experience. Even in representational work, the artist and the viewer have to ask questions like, "Why is she sad?" or "What is she going to do?" These questions imply the influence of history and future over the figure. When my abstract form became the focus, each shape represented an individual in the present and it became possible for me to see more than what I knew about myself. Through this process, I began to realize that I was part of a larger form. I could remove the control issue and cease the struggle toward the future. I could create space for the present inside myself by allowing the variety of my experiences and relationships to coexist without one having more influence than another. My understanding of the present grew larger. I found that it is not about stopping or making an "I am" statement. It is about relationships between individuals.

I moved into a new house with a large studio. It was close to town, close to schools and stores, and close to people. I rejoined the world.

Lesson 11

Critique can be terrifying. It is also one of the artist's greatest tools. At some point we are going to have to let our work go out into the world where others will experience their own interaction with our sculptures, with our expressions and, ultimately, with us. Feedback from others is a critical part of the artistic process. As we evaluate our work and the work of others it is important that we remain objective.

Critique is an opportunity for dialog that will promote greater self-awareness and a stronger sculptural expression. The object is to learn from each other and to tighten our individual expression so that we can take our work to the next level. Always be honest in a critique, be kind with your comments, and be receptive to the opinions of others.

CHAPTER 11

My new house had a huge studio with heat and running water. It was close to my kids' school and there were other children in the neighborhood. I felt like we had, indeed, rejoined the world. I had a good job working as the director of youth programs for a community service organization. My home was alive with people. On Saturdays, a group of my friends – an ex-con, a PhD, and a former stripper, among others – gathered with me in my studio to work and converse with plenty of dark beer and cigarettes on the side. Through a thread of conversation that never got too tangled, we had laughter and resolution, dirty jokes and wry humor, and awareness that what we were doing while we modeled the wax was important, sacred, and inviolable.

I had finished *Now* and moved on – further into the realms of abstraction. My work became more architectural as I fought the figurative influence. A sculpture that had been about the process of mind somehow morphed into a buffalo, a football, and a cave dwelling before it was finished enough to be placed on the shelf, melt in the heat, and never be fixed again.

For many years, I had thought that communication was about trying to get other people to understand my point of view. My conversations had been about hearing myself think. I had never done a lot of listening, although I was especially adept at extracting fragments from another person's speech to further my own intentions. The group that gathered in my studio every week changed my opinion. The dialog and the relationships were richer and more rewarding when each person had the freedom to contribute. Then the variety of ideas and emotions attached to our thread of conversation broadened our personal perspectives. For the first time, dialog was not debate. Winning the argument or making the final point only left me stuck in my own knowledge.

It took a long time for this awareness to hit home because initially, I had been their teacher. Then a student asked me if I started each piece by conceiving of the geometric shapes or if I discovered them after the work was in progress. When she looked me in the eye, I recognized the passion and drive I had experienced when I apprenticed at the foundry. I also saw in her the love of the work and her fear of failure. And, like me, I saw a woman trying to come to terms with herself while attempting to touch something greater. The honesty in her expression was like a shock, reverberating through my layers of self-protection and self-absorption and I had to respond with integrity. I confessed I didn't know the answer. She laughed and lit a cigarette. Then she became both my student and my friend. That was the beginning of the dialog and the opening of another door at the edge of my awareness.

We all wanted to know how to ask the right question. That meant that we had to examine all the questions, weigh them and chew on them, so we could determine what the right question was. If we found it, we could figure out how to ask it, and then our dreams might come true. The dynamic in my studio occurred through the conviction that each of us was ultimately responsible for our own fate. We were looking for a crystal ball that would guide us in our choices to a moment of peace that stretched to infinity. Each of us defined peace in a different way.

David was a tall, highly skilled craftsman frustrated with his previous artistic attempts. He thought he would try sculpture and, by extension, coalesce the various facets of himself into a single identity. He believed the ideal life was that of the guy who owned the local hardware store. That guy was content in his job as well as his domestic life – secure in the knowledge that life would flow, albeit slowly, in smooth transition day to day until death. In that flow, he would encounter myriad individuals, each presenting their own problem that he would help to solve through his intricate knowledge of the odds and ends in his maze of shelves and boxes. Through his success as the solver of problems, he could measure his own validity and be at peace. David didn't make a lot of art in the studio. Instead, he built pedestals, crafted bases, and joined us in the conversation.

Belinda was a German woman obsessed with astrology and quietly proud of her previous foray into topless dancing. She hated noise and heavy lifting, yet she drove four hours every Saturday to be with us in that garage. She believed she had the ideal life, or that it was at least within her grasp. She had a house in the tropics, her studio was almost complete, and she had money in the bank. For her, peace was about touching lives on the edge and about an identity borrowed or created that gave her a place to hide secrets and grow power.

Lynn was the student who first became my friend. She had left a tenured teaching position at a respected university to move to Santa Fe and be an artist. At the time, her journey seemed to be about confronting and freeing herself from blocks. She was especially hard on herself and she was driven. Sculpture and dialog were the pupas from which she would emerge as a fully formed butterfly. She wanted freedom, acceptance, and success.

There were others that frequented our sessions, but mostly they fluttered on the fringes offering morsels that helped us move the conversation forward rather than actively participating in it. We were all stuck in the same place when we started. We all wanted to reconcile our lives in the world with the life inside of us, and the studio was a place where it could happen – at least for one day a week.

We brought everything to the table on those Saturday afternoons. Love, sex, children, jobs, fears, triumphs, belief systems and ideologies were the meat that fueled our conversations. Our souls were naked on the table, posed for examination. The afternoons stretched into years and the studio became our confessional, complete with sacred rites and fervent prayer.

Linda Ronstadt, Willie Nelson, and Crystal Gayle tapes ate their way around the dirty spools of a twenty-dollar cassette player, and wax vapor rose from an old electric frying pan. The studio stank of cigarette smoke, empty beer bottles, and burnt hair caught in the recycled wax. Patina chemicals, propane torches, and dirty laundry next to the washing machine occupied their own space, while my dog perpetually tangled himself around the worktable.

The dog barked and the kids wanted us to watch them on the trampoline. The telephone rang and old pickup trucks hauled moss rock, piñon trees, flagstones, and land-scaping timbers for sale into the bare, dirt-brown expanse of the yard. Our conversation was frequently interrupted, giving us pause to consider other perspectives. The unforeseen breaks renewed the dialog and kept it alive.

The verity of our declarations was questioned and our convictions were witnessed during those long afternoons. Lynn would put down her tool, lift her beer and say, "Wait, say that again, say it in a different way," and I would have to think about it and try again to finish the thought or make sense out of it. More often than not, we would laugh because I couldn't remember what I had just said; the words had been coming too fast. We thought we needed a tape recorder to document all the threads. At times, we thought we were brilliant. We knew we were fighting against ourselves, yet we empathized with each other when one of us ripped apart a piece that had taken weeks to create, forcing the sculptor to put the wax back in the pan and start over again.

The dialog required us to act because failure to do so meant either a lack of courage or false expression. And despite the chaos of barking dogs, the clamor of kids playing, ringing telephones, and the noisy cycles of the washing machine, we each experienced transformations. The thread of the dialog centered on the philosophy of art and incorporated elements of language theory, pop psychology, history, and the critique of work. But the thing that kept us honest was the work itself. The sculptures brought with them a reaching toward something and a desire to know. Each piece was a question of faith and the critique process provided an element of temptation, the opportunity to renege on a particular belief or, through conviction, spread the gospel.

Like spider webs in a small space, our lives spun and crossed, becoming, at times, indistinguishable as unique threads. And in our web – woven of dreams and failures, hope and determination – the rudiments of individual experience were ensnared, suspended, and isolated until we could devour them and reach resolution. When we met, we took turns playing spider and fly. We alternated identities until a problem was solved, a block was removed and our sculptures were freed from their own weights and able to move again.

We looked at our motivations – what we were trying to gain and why, as well as what the conflicts were in ourselves. And when the revelation of personal experience was too intense and beyond words, we looked at shape theory, geometric forms and internal symbols to create a space for objectivity in a highly charged emotional room.

Often before we were ready, and sometimes against our will, the work evolved and propelled us forward. We moved through a kaleidoscope of symbols and days, creating our gods and spinning our lives. Buzzed on beer and drunk on conversation, we thought we had asked the right questions. Then each of us was forced to live the convictions of our answers and act according to our faith.

Lesson 12

Executing our work with conviction is the most important aspect of the sculptural process. If the work is sloppy, no one will be interested in what we are trying to express. When we are sure of ourselves, the work speaks with certainty and our viewers will respond to the whole of the piece instead of imperfections in the detail.

As we near the end of this process and begin to finish our sculptures, we have to make it look like any imperfections are deliberate. We execute every geometric form and every relationship with intent. If our work is primarily a triangle, then it needs to be a triangle. It must have a sharp apex and definitive lines between points – even if those lines are created through negative space – otherwise, it will be a "maybe" and will speak only our own doubt about what the triangle represents. We cannot express hope and inspiration or exhilaration and freedom if we do not complete the sides of the triangle or define the apex.

At this point, we have to recognize that we will not resolve every problem in these particular sculptures. We must work on bringing the pieces home by executing every plane, surface, and shape with conviction, saving the problems we cannot resolve for the next piece. Ultimately, these problems will formulate our next questions.

CHAPTER 12

My faith revolved around language. Language was the godhead from which all knowledge of self and the world evolved. The languages of spoken and written words, body language, and geometric symbolism were all roads I traveled – touching and tasting more than the small, one-stoplight-town of my own experience.

From my earliest childhood memories, I remember my father asking, "How can I know what I think until I see what I say?" – taken from E.M. Forester. For me, this question carried a lot of weight. It was his only response to my poetry, temper-tantrums, fights with my siblings, and loneliness in school. Rather than engage in debate or a battle of wills, he would throw this question at me, making me responsible for the fact that my thoughts, emotions, actions and reactions were incomplete. He would entertain my ideas and passion only after I had revealed to myself the essence or underlying meaning of my expression. From him, I understood that something was alive behind the words – not merely emotion, not only memory –

and that I needed to dig deep within myself in order to see it.

This question became my motto. It was the impetus for my drive and the motivation for my future. My father had died too soon – before he taught me how to see what I was saying and before I could interact with him as a whole person.

After he died, I had no method of adapting this question to my life, so I reworded it to my level of understanding. I translated the question to read, "How can I know what I think until I *hear* what I say?" In turn, I talked incessantly to anyone who gave even the slightest appearance of listening to me. Through talking, I could see the response to my words in the face and body of my listeners and could fine-tune my verbal expression to alter their physical reaction. I could have an impact.

Before my life evolved, I had been trapped in a silent world. I had been isolated in a town where I knew no one and my husband, when he wasn't working, watched TV. The circumstances of my life pushed me to transform that question again. This time, the original asking was intact, but the meaning had more to do with artistic expression. Sculpture became the visual manifestation of my thoughts, though at the time I could not readily interpret what I was saying.

I knew that the relationships between verbal languages could facilitate a greater understanding of a particular expression. I had studied Latin and Greek mythology in school and through them my knowledge of words had deepened. For example, I loved knowing where the word *amorous* came from and how the word *panic* had evolved. Ancient languages were my secret entrance to a world still filled with magic. As a child, I believed that Greek gods were alive – hiding in trees and underwater, in music and behind my words.

I wanted to find similar relationships in the methods of visual expression so I could finally see what I was saying. There had to be roots – something that tied these relationships together – unveiling an origin that transcended culture and had a history. I wanted to see the common threads that would form a context for understanding. In short, I was determined to find the meaning behind surface interpretation of visual language. It was this conviction that prompted me to develop the shape theory. Through all of those Saturdays, however, I realized that my shape theory was incomplete. I had not yet traveled the distance with it.

One Friday night in early spring, David and his wife came to dinner. I had just returned from a business trip and David had just prepped a canvas for a new painting. We were talking about words because David typically incorporated text into his painting to further the meaning of his work. But he never believed the written component was successful – intellectually or emotionally. He knew the writing was a crutch too weak to support the failure of his brush. For this new canvas, David wanted to paint a picture about rapture, but he didn't know where to start.

We were drinking scotch and catching up on our lives. David and I were humming with a feeling inspired by the sultry air, alcohol and impassioned conversation. I was fascinated by his choice of subject and wanted to know what he meant by rapture. He couldn't verbalize it for me so we looked up the definition in a dictionary. The literal definition of rapture didn't excite us, but the root meaning of the word did. The root revealed things we had not associated with the word. *Raptus* is the root for rapture. It is also the root for raptor and rapt. Furthermore, raptus is a bird of prey and is associated with the verb "to seize."

Suddenly, rapture existed for us as something far larger than what we had known. The inherent meaning of the word could shift according to our understanding of the action associated with it. One could be enraptured when seized and carried away by a bird of prey. Such an experience could be dangerous and/or desirable.

I had been reading Jorge Luis Borge's book *Seven Nights* and was excited about what he said about words. David and I began to talk about it. We needed to know what Borges meant when he said that words are an aesthetic because, as we delved into the word *rapture*, we recognized ourselves as lost. The world existed through our definitions of the words we used to describe it and our definitions were no longer solid. Our use of words had become static. Definitions based on habit and convenience had replaced our childhood wonder and our casual use of them had killed the magic. On this night, rapture brought the magic back and we were not going to let it slip away again. As artists, we thought we could hold on to our understanding and pursuit of the aesthetic. We were wrong.

We found that the term "aesthetic" derives its meaning from the Greek word *aisthetikos*, which means a sense of perception. Beauty is about perception, as are words. Their aesthetic is derived through the multitude of definitions associated with each of them. Language is not truth. Interaction with language speaks truth because words are like sculptures. They create equal opportunity for intersections and shadows.

Later that night, after the scotch was gone and the children were in bed, the possibilities of what we had discussed hit me like an electric current. I knew what I had to do. I would take words out of their two-dimensional, linear cages and put them into three-dimensional form. I would explore words through sculpture. I would examine the aesthetic of words through art. I would sculpt a poem.

I took the premise that each letter has a geometric shape and the relationship between these shapes in a word is no different from the relationship between shapes in a sculpture. The first sculpture was *Act*. As I worked the piece, I explored the definitions associated with the word and located fifteen different meanings. I wanted to understand how that many definitions could relate to the geometric symbolism of its letters and their relationship to each other. A triangle, an incomplete circle and a Christian cross were the shapes that formed the piece. Together, they spoke to the process of metamorphosis through conscious risk-taking. The sculpture became a representation of an attempt to transform or transcend oneself and revealed that the word "act" implies faith and requires courage.

Until that point, the studio had been a comfortable place. Ideas and people blew through like the warm wind in late spring and early summer – soothing and poignant with possibilities. Traces of them left a thin film that coated everything, changed the appearance of surfaces but made no serious impact. As I worked on *Act*, I became crazed – caught in a swirling storm with powerful momentum.

I was not looking at what it meant *to* act, I was looking at the thing itself, at what act is. Day after day the word stared me down, reflecting in its form the history of my fear and the future of my faith. It echoed in my thoughts, in my dialog, in my sleep. Act. Just act. The dark tunnels between and behind the letters came together and became a form of their own, reminiscent of Stonehenge or the monolithic heads on Easter Island. It was like an ancient commandment that could not be ignored. Nor could it be placed on a shelf and forgotten.

I was on fire. The shape theory had been my armature and guide for eight years, but I had never built a sculpture based solely on its principles. As I formed these letters – in my head, on paper, and in the wax – my passion was ignited and my imagination was limitless. Triangles and ovals were not implied or drawn through negative space by my mind. They were real, solid things in the sculpture that fully expressed the emotional symbolism I suggested in my shape theory. But it was the darkness at the intersection of planes that excited me the most. The sculpture was more human than any figure I had ever created. It illuminated the process of my mind. The subconscious ooze of collective memory and emotion was alive in the shadows between and behind the letters. The letters – recognizable as both letters and shapes – were wrought with predictable symbolism that paved the way for conscious interpretation. The theory was no longer a theory. I had applied it to three-dimensional form.

I understood that an object is an object only according to the way I define it. When I encounter a wall as a child, I know the wall is solid and I cannot pass through it. Later, when my understanding evolves through the process of my experience, I know that if I hit the wall with enough force it will break. The wall is no longer solid. It is merely a temporary barrier I accept as solid because it makes me feel safe. Moreover, I can repair the wall so that the illusion of it being impenetrable remains. But I can no longer define it in the same way. The wall is solid only in relation to other objects.

Solid is no longer a static truth and my definition of the wall is merely a manifestation of my desire. I do not change my definition for everyday use, but I am aware that the definition I use is not always true. *Act* made me confront the fact that my understanding of myself is limited by my need to protect the illusions I create through my definitions.

In the time it took to finish *Act*, everyone in the studio worked harder, faster and more intensely than we had ever done before. We not only sculpted wax, we ate it, inhaled it, and oozed it from our pores like sweat – rancid and slightly sweet. *Act* inspired all of us. Everyone participated in its critique and celebrated the dialog that surrounded it. Dancing around the sculpture and pacing back and forth on the sticky concrete floor, we shared a steady stream of ideas through the telling of life stories and the recounting of dreams; we knew that we would act. Our jobs as hygienist, program director, astrologer, and shop manager had made us just "wannabees" and that definition no longer served. We had learned how to build walls and knock them down. *Act* had evoked awareness that everything we had been doing until then had been simply practice or play. Now it was time to get serious and to take our understanding and expression to the next level.

So we planned, schemed and stopped working long enough to crunch numbers and write a tentative business plan to open a joint studio. We were willing to risk everything to make a living selling our work. Grabbing hands, we jumped up and down, laughed, whooped, and hugged each other with the realization that we no longer wanted to be artists – we were artists. It was time to introduce us to the world.

Lesson 13

*W*e have been talking about the particular emotional symbolism of each shape and how the relationship between shapes constitutes expression in three-dimensional art. Now we must explore the descriptive capabilities of shapes more fully.

We all know what an apple looks like, but each apple has characteristics that denote its particular individuality. These characteristics occur internally and are not readily visible in the roundness of its form. Therefore, when we sculpt the apple we must render more than its surface. Using other shapes to create the primary form will help us recognize that our surface impressions are illusions. There is more to be explored and then expressed about an apple than what first meets our eye. Using different shapes as adjectives to describe the form gives us the opportunity to glean other, and perhaps more relevant, perspectives on our subjects and will provide us with the tools to express those perspectives with conviction.

CHAPTER 13

We lost David. Over the course of a couple months, he stopped coming to the studio. Initially, he said that he didn't like my sculpture because it was too architectural and too clean. There was not enough texture to it and its lines were too sharp. He thought it was massive and heavy. Then he missed a few Saturdays. He told us that he had to finish designing new sets at work and needed to spend more time at home. He had bought a new house and felt he had to build a fence for the dog and insulate his garage so he would have a place to paint.

I didn't understand why he was disappearing. For almost two years, David and his wife had been a mainstay in my life. We shared the same values and struggled with the same issues – how to simultaneously be a parent and an artist, how to live in the world without compromising or prostituting ourselves, how to make enough money to survive in Santa Fe, and still have time for the things and people who were really important. Our kids were best friends, our houses were close to each other, and we spent all our free time together both in and out of the studio. Suddenly, they didn't want their son playing with mine anymore and David was gone from the studio like he had never been there at all. I was devastated. It didn't make sense. I had thought we were friends. I thought the connection between us was real and that I knew who he was.

Lynn and I spent hours trying to figure out what had happened and did our best to excuse his actions and forgive him. But I was hurt, confused and not ready to let David go. We had made plans. We were going into our future with conviction. We were *Act* personified. And then he quit, just left without even saying goodbye, without justification or remorse, gone.

After my heart had settled, my first inclination was to call David a coward – fearful of becoming a true artist and living his dream. In my mind, I linked David with my father who I believed was afraid of failure – afraid of being less than the best. He had a block that lasted for years and wouldn't admit it. He wrote some – dabbling with words on paper like David dabbled with them on canvas – but he didn't work at it. My father didn't make art the determining factor in how he lived his life. It was a sidebar or maybe a lingering memory of who he had once been, but it was not who he had become. He was, at death, more a business-man than an artist, a sometimes-father and a sometimes-husband, a social player with skewed priorities. Ultimately, I felt that my father had lived a lie and had died in it. I condemned David to the same understanding and tried to work again, but I could not. David's reaction to my sculpture was nagging at me. I couldn't ignore it or let it pass by writing him off as a coward incapable of acting. In addition, I had always valued his critique of my work.

I kept fiddling with *Act*, adding texture and taking it off, breaking up the planes and playing with color. I had missed something about its meaning, but I was afraid to take the sculpture apart to find it. I wanted to believe in my understanding of this word because it indicated the arrival of reconciliation between my life as an artist and my life as a mother. What I didn't realize was that I was looking at the sculpture from a limited perspective.

As Lynn, Belinda and I talked on those Saturday afternoons after David had left, I was forced to deal with the part of the sculpture I didn't like. I was stuck on the letter A. It seemed to sit on the rest of the sculpture like a mask. I didn't understand how *Act* could be partly a mask or a pretense. I tried to shrug off the question and talked about acts in a play and performers acting. I thought about how actors must become the role they play in order to convince the audience of a true expression. Then, suddenly, I understood. The first part of an act is the determination of the role and the donning of its costume. We choose our roles, don our costumes, and begin to become who we want to be. It is a choice and we live within its process – not its consequence.

My father was a Southern man who had experienced poverty and instability as a child. During the Great Depression, Chalmers, my grandfather, moved from job to job with family in tow through the small, dry counties of Alabama and numerous little towns pockmarked by violence and fear. My father seldom talked of the day-to-day experience. Instead, he told me of the time Chalmers was the local sheriff and a rock came crashing through the window of their house because Chalmers had tried to shut down an illegal still. Talking about his childhood, my father told me how his brothers threw him off a bridge into a river to teach him to swim and when he rose to the surface a water moccasin was staring him in the face. He swam not because he was afraid of drowning but because he was afraid of the snake. And he told me, again and again, the story of his grandfather, Bud, who dressed in black and wore pearl-handled pistols on his hips. In 1924, Bud died in a gunfight – ambushed by a lie and the promise of a truce, he was found riddled with bullets in Heron, Illinois.

I felt that my father identified more with the people who lived before him than those who filled his life. He saw beauty in them and believed that their lives were larger than the picture their actions painted. As a child, he had lived in terror of a father who drank too much and cursed at life. Never-the-less, his father always managed to ensure that there was a piano in the house. His mother played the piano, raised the children, and found herself repeatedly packing dishes as they moved from one over-crowded house to another. His much-older brothers tied him to a tree so he couldn't tag along. Always, he remembered wanting to be a part of something bigger. He created romance and reason from his tragedy and consequently held onto it dearly.

My father told me that after his father killed himself, he was kicked out of five different schools for fighting. He fought with the other boys because they called him a sissy for his love of classical music and books. By fighting back, he defended his manhood and gave credibility to those things that were, for him, more meaningful than fast cars, rock-and-roll, and small-town gossip.

In so many ways, I looked at my father from the perspective of a child and hated him for selling out. He talked about art but failed as an artist. His love affairs, loud parties and premature death had shaped then shattered my world. He left without saying goodbye, without justification or remorse, just gone. I detested him for being so important that I did not know who I was without him. I needed to condemn him, to shrink him down so that I could be bigger than him, stand on my own two feet and recreate my world.

Then there was *Act*, the loss of David, and the memory of my father showing the world that he was a man – a strong man who stood up, climbed out, and ultimately provided for his family while he pursued his dream.

David was also a Southern man from a poor family. He too wanted to be a father, husband, and provider who brought home more than a paycheck. He loved his wife and he loved his child. He wanted to have a family in the conventional sense – unlike what he had experienced as a child. He acted on that desire not in pursuit of art, fame, or money, but to live with intent.

Over the months in the studio, *Act* inspired me to recognize that my actions had created a distinct pattern in my life – a tapestry of day-to-day experiences woven with hope. I thought the dialog surrounding the sculpture required me to make a choice. I had to decide if I would continue to weave the same pattern or if I would interject a bold design and new colors into the fabric, changing the way I defined myself and lived my life.

I realized that David, like my father, had decided to weave the same pattern and to make his life into art. He left because there was no room in my studio for his decision. Lynn, Belinda and I had decided that art and intellect would determine our daily lives. Finally, I understood that the concept of *act*, in its multitude of definitions, was not about a linear trajectory toward the realization of dreams. Through the sculpture and the lost relationship with David, I realized the masks we conjured for ourselves and the roles we played in the world were manifestations of our desires. I understood that when we become bigger than we once were, we recognize in ourselves the essence of who we have always been. Our growth is not a departure. It is an expansion. I finished the sculpture, put it away, and started sculpting the next word of the poem.

Lesson 14

*I*n Africa, there is a tribe called Shona. They are sculptors and their work is an attempt to express religious conviction through the physical manipulation of sculptural media. They believe that their work comes alive and that, upon completion, it will exist as an individual in the world. One of the early Shona sculptors, Joram Mariga, said, "One should avoid realism in sculpture – create a large place for the brain and large eyes because sculptures are beings that must be able to think and see for themselves for eternity."

We must take into account the fact that our work exists beyond our creative influence. As we sculpt, we nurture our work and endow it with life. Like a child, the work will grow under our care until it is able to stand on its own; and when it does, it will be beyond our reach. Consequently, we must make every attempt to guide our work into supportive relationships.

We need to think about placement. Is this an indoor work or an outdoor work? Will it require a base or a pedestal? How will the presentation enhance or hinder our geometric expression? Does our sculpture need lots of space around it or will it dialog well with other objects close by? We need to take it out of the context of its origin and examine it in other environments so that we get a sense of what it will become once it leaves our hands.

CHAPTER 14

I understood that I needed to act with intent so I charged ahead – barreling into my future like a Mack truck racing down the highway. I was goal-oriented, oblivious to the effects of my momentum and unstoppable. The loss of David and the completion of *Act* were sobering. Those two events made me reevaluate the speed and force of my actions and realize that I was always acting. But I was unable to ascertain the concrete effects of my actions in life because it seemed that whenever I reached a particular plateau there was another one looming over me, beckoning me to climb again. I had to slow down and temper the fury about how I understood act – that act is not final, not the ultimate purpose to, or the result of a process. Act is a process and process is infinite. 'Act on' became the first line of the poem and when *On* was finished I put both words together on the table.

Magic occurs when two forms interact with one another and reveal through their union the force of something greater and more significant than each. It is a calming thing, awesome and still. On the table together, *Act* and *On* created that magic. The parallel and repetitive planes of each word coalesced into a new form by themselves. Witnessing this event, Lynn, Belinda, and I were momentarily still. *Act On* emerged as a complete work, more complete than the individual words that formed it. Together, as a single sculptural expression, they were powerful and at peace, resulting in a deep breath in my studio and in my life.

Through sculpture, I had pursued art spelled with a capital A – the real thing, a first-rate expression not sullied by dishonesty, sentiment, or the influence of others. Art was something I felt I had not yet created and maybe never would. Despite being driven by determination, conviction, and the need to make sense out of my world, my destination was not clearly defined. Art was the amalgam of all my desires, but I would never fully grasp it for it was ever changing, both in process and product. Art was knowable only through the changing perspectives from which my interaction with it occurred. I needed to understand what was constant and what in the creative process was relevant to my direction so that my actions in life were recognizably intentional. Only then could I act with integrity. In the heat of late July, I started the third word and the next line of the poem.

Faith was something I had questioned for most of my life. I felt the need for something solid, something to stand on – a base or an anchor to keep me grounded. My adult memories of my father are selective in sustaining an illusion of him that allows me to live with myself. In these memories, he is smaller than I knew him to be – afraid, running and raging at life, as well as at my mother and himself. I imagine him as overly critical, extremely judgmental, and an abuser who belittled women and children to avoid confronting his failures.

But as a child, I had faith in the construct of my father's world. In those childhood memories of him I envisaged a very different man. In that picture, my father built a framework for living that was as real as my nightmares and as strong as his arms around me when I was afraid. We read books and climbed to the roof of the house to talk about them and watch the sunsets. The jazz beat of his piano playing filled our home. Hunched over the keyboard in a flannel shirt and black leather vest, he bobbed his head to the rhythm of the music. As always, a cigarette hung out of the corner of his mouth and the smoke wreathed above his head, blending with the steam that rose from his coffee. When he caught sight of me he would grin, revealing the missing teeth that had been knocked out playing football as a teenager. He would call me to him and ask me to sing "My Funny Valentine." He smiled at my efforts and told me to sing my way and from my heart because imitating someone else's version was not worthy of me. He was strong enough to hold onto, strong enough to be my hero, and strong enough to give meaning to a life that was constantly changing.

The void that existed following my father's death was suddenly more present than ever. My father's books – standing dormant on their shelves – gathered dust. His clothes were put in boxes. The jazz albums of Oscar Peterson, John Coltrane, Stan Getz, and Thelonius Monk were replaced with Sade and Dolly Parton. The piano was silent.

Our house grew cold. If I saw beauty in the sunset, I did not share it with anyone because the words no longer held significance. My father had been my touchstone for knowledge and understanding. With his death, only his words remained in my head. But at the time, the words were not strong enough to hold me up and give me definition. They were not strong enough to hold up a world without him and, as such, they were empty. The words became a lie.

He once told me about the existential leap of faith, the suspension of the ethical and the metaphysical plunge into the dark void of unarticulated experience. His words had left a bitter taste of cold metal in my mouth. The questions that circled around this stuff of faith were nearly impossible to digest because faith was a foreign substance, not kin to the soft, moveable thing that was me without him.

In high school, my friends and I read the "Book of Job" and I discussed its philosophical ramifications with the sure mind of adolescence, using words my father taught me – words not yet familiar to me. I learned that the last part of the story – when Job gets everything back sevenfold – had been added centuries after the original text was written. The whole concept of reward and punishment felt artificial to me, a trick contrived to keep people sane or at least docile. God had left Job on the dung heap covered in boils and grieving loss, his ears ringing with the thunderous voice in the whirlwind that comforted none and gave nothing. And still, Job was expected to keep the faith – which he did – but why?

As a teenager and young adult, that question kept me hopping. It was a wonderful bit of philosophical fodder to roll around on my tongue as though I was God – capable not only of answering the question, but responsible for its conception. I thought I knew the dung heap because I heard the voice of my father from the whirlwind, his words thundering in my head. I thought I was like Job because I saw myself as ugly and felt the pain of inexperience, insecurity, and loss. Then, there came the realization that there is no answer to the question without living Job's life and knowing his god. My understanding of Job could only come through the perspective of self-experience and no matter how apt Job's dung heap may have seemed as a metaphor, it was not my dung heap. So where is faith? And how do you hold it after you find it? And for what purpose if it has no reason for being and doesn't solve anything?

"Act on faith." There isn't a question in this three-word statement nor is there much meaning. Those three words are like saying, "lean on wall" except that we at least have an idea about what constitutes a wall. A wall is a concrete object. We can build one and knock it down. But faith is just a word. Even the dictionary isn't conclusive in defining faith. It implies that faith is about fidelity, keeping one's promises, or loyalty to God. It says that faith means believing in something for which there is no proof. Faith is about trust. But the root for faith is the same root for the word *bide*, which means to continue in a state or condition, to continue in a place, to wait confidently or defiantly. So how does one "act on faith" if act means movement, process, and becoming while faith signifies waiting and is still?

I remembered working on my sculpture *In Time* and how I felt when I understood that only through forgiveness could I suspend my past, cease its effect on me and exercise my will. At that time, I believed an act of free will was a metaphysical suicide that I was incapable of performing. Forgiving my past meant obliterating my knowledge of myself and I could not let that part of me die. I thought that I would condemn myself to a pattern of spirals repeating itself throughout time. I was like those trees in the park with my children – rooted in the ground of my experience and unable to change the nature of me without ceasing to be me.

The statement "Act on faith" seemed to convey a sense of false hope. *In Time* demonstrated that to act, one must forgive and suspend the past, cut away everything solid and everything knowable through definition. That includes one's knowledge of self, faith, family, and history. One cannot act *on* anything – one can only "act on."

The sculpture grew like a tangled weed – a thick spiral of letters in a tight, tornadic form that collapsed in places compressed by its own weight. It was a cage around emptiness. FAITH, in capital letters, was the beginning of a new sentence instead of the end. "Act on. Faith…

Lesson 15

As artists, we want to find the inherent meaning in our subject. That pursuit gives rise to process. Process provides opportunities for further examination through new or expanded definitions. Process is as infinite as our ability and desire to question. But at some point we have to accept our work as finished so we can move forward in life and engage with a new subject that also hints at the inherent meaning we pursue. But how do we know when the work is complete, and the process taken as far as it can go?

Close your eyes and slowly run your hands over the entire surface of your sculpture. What do you feel? Are you satisfied with the physical sensations? Do they bring you pleasure? Can you identify the emotion this touching evokes in you? Open your eyes and look at your work. Does the feeling you get from touching the sculpture stay true, or does it get lost in what you know about your work when made visible? What is the relationship between your silent, tantric knowledge of touching in the dark and your light-filled consciousness? Are they the same, leaving you silent and still in your relationship to the work? If so, then the work is complete. If the meanings of your experiences remain irreconcilable – take it apart and begin again.

CHAPTER 15

My friends and I tried to define faith as we worked long hours past the fading light of late summer evenings. I was coming at it from a philosophical perspective, looking for a definition similar to how one looks for a puzzle piece – trying this and that and getting frustrated when a piece didn't fit. My mother had grown up in a Jewish home and my father was raised a Southern Baptist. Neither of them practiced their religions. Consequently, I had never been formally trained in what faith was supposed to be according to the prescribed conventions of organized religions. And yet, I believed in it, was consumed by it – I just didn't understand what it was. Faith seemed to be both a value and an object and, as such, it was a paradox.

One does not say "Act on love" or "Act on anger." One says, "Act out of love" or, "He acted out of anger" because each of these abstract concepts is experienced as a state of being. If faith were trust, then faith would be a verb, as well as a noun. But one cannot say, "I faith you." Instead, one says "I have faith in you." Faith is a noun, an object, and a verb transitive – a connection between things. It is what happens at the point of intersection. It is the deepest shadow and I wanted to shine a light on that dark place and *see* what was there.

Lynn came at a definition through rebellion, prompted in large part from her background. She was from the Midwest and had been raised a thundering Protestant with church events three times a week and all day Sunday and a "don't stray from the path" daily admonishment. For years, she hated the idea of God because the God she knew couldn't love her.

Belinda could not find a definition at all. Her native language was German and she said there was no word for faith. The closest term to it is trust. But trust isn't faith and what is faith if you never experienced the word except as a witness to someone else's culture?

Belinda talked a lot about her father and her childhood while we worked. She was sculpting two creatures. One was a huge and horrible monster; the other was kin to a girl in braids. The figures were physically connected where their hands would be, and it appeared that the monster was swinging the girl around. From some angles, the girl looked to be enjoying the moment, thrilled by the intensity between falling and flying that occurred simultaneously in the spinning experience. From other angles, the monster was pulling the girl toward itself, hunched over and ready to devour her while she pulled away, twisting and squirming in opposition.

Belinda told us about Germany, where everything is neat and square. She told of how her father insisted that she mow the lawn in straight lines despite her urge to push the machine in crazy patterns. Such an act of defiance would have obliterated the crisp, linear definitions that imprisoned her as a child. She said her father was a quiet man and she was desperately afraid of him – more so because of his subdued manner. She would have preferred to see him yell and scream because she felt something ugly and out of control behind his firm insistence and governed façade. That feeling formed the terror that fed her nightmares.

"Oh yah, we went to church and everything, but I don't think that's what you're talking about here," Belinda said. "No, that's not faith as I think you mean it. Germans aren't like you." I wanted to know what she meant by that. If Germans weren't like me or if Belinda wasn't like me, who and what made us so different? I had known people and families whose lives were highly structured. They existed behind a mask, which barely concealed a high-pitched hysteria that sent me barking and whining like a dog responding to an inaudible pitch.

Lynn thought she knew what Belinda was talking about. Her childhood experience also contained an austere perspective; and while her lawn was not the metaphor she would choose to describe false order and profane piety, she had another. Church suppers were the worst, she said. Everyone came all dressed up and cheerful with a dish to pass. The covered dish of food was placed next to other dishes on a long table. Her mother worried about how her dish would be received in comparison to the other potluck offerings. Would it be accepted or ignored by other parishioners? And worse were the deacons and deacons' wives who looked down long noses at you like they were sniffing out improprieties. If they detected something amiss, they were determined to identify its source, root it out, and reveal it for what it was.

I imagined Lynn at these gatherings, round and blue-eyed, worrying that her feet were too big and masking her intelligence in small, quick smiles. I envisioned her avoiding intimacy or eye contact, walking behind people, gathering her perceived physical immensity into a tight bundle that could not help but draw attention to her resulting lack of inherent grace. She was the only girl out of four children, and she knew she would be judged and talked about like the covered dish on the table. I ached for her.

We talked about piety and how it was a false thing, foreign to faith. But as we talked, we got no closer to understanding. We could articulate what faith is not, but could not say what it is. We tried next to examine ourselves in relationship to our faith. We imagined ourselves – and faith – as solid objects, where the relationship was the important thing. Up to this point, that's what we had discovered through our dialog.

I became increasingly frustrated. It was hot in the studio and I hadn't used an armature to construct the piece I was working on. I would leave it at night after a long day of work and return the next morning only to find that the upper part of the letter F had melted and fallen off the sculpture and onto the floor. I would have to reattach it and patiently wait as the hot, new wax cooled and formed a bond. Each day, the sculpture sank a little more into itself until the bottom of it was riddled with bulging lines like the legs of an elephant, thick and wrinkled. I spent more time fixing the damage from the heat than actually sculpting the form. And yet, through all of the surgeries, the form stayed relatively intact. Needless to say, each repair changed it slightly, such that the F wasn't quite in the same place and the base didn't have the same dance-like grace to which I had aspired. But unlike other works that had undergone the same process, this piece seemed to benefit and evolve from its numerous resurrections.

The days were getting shorter and we became more dependent on artificial light. We were also forced to shut the garage door due to the bite of cooler evenings. *Faith* was on the table and it was tall. I could not see the planes in the way I needed to without the sunlight. I rigged another shop lamp to the ceiling and the light shone down the empty spiral of the form, illuminating its center. I sat down, put my feet up on the table and tilted back in the chair, which gave me a new perspective. The sculpture was positioned so that my gaze rested on the lower half of the letter A and there was a trickle of light that flowed like water down one of the legs. My eyes followed the light up the leg and behind the line that crossed the triangle into the interior of the work. I called the others over, pointed out the light stream, and asked them what they saw. Lynn understood. The form of *Faith* was dark, a shadow. The light existed only in the negative space of the interior.

Belinda didn't see it. We tried to explain it to her conceptually; faith is a solid object and we exist inside it as the thing that can't be defined. The relationship was important, but not in the way we had thought. Faith defines us, not the other way around. Faith is. We become. And we are capable of becoming only in faith. Faith is the vessel that contains the free-flowing substance that is us.

Belinda still didn't get it. I said that we all live within the construct of a particular thing we call faith. Her experience in Germany, Lynn's in the Midwest, and mine in New Mexico all formed in each of us an individual faith that now, in this studio, we shared with each other. Our faith is our conviction that something exists that can give meaning to our lives. And when we peruse the art on Canyon Road, we are no better than the church deacons and no worse because, like them, we are afraid of anything that might reveal our faith as less than the totality of truth. Without faith, we have no reason for being.

How we choose to live day-to-day is the manifestation of our desire to touch and fill the form of our faith. Consequently, faith is the driving force that dictates our actions in the world. We do not choose our faith. It does not evolve as we do. It is always there and always recognizable in spite of the limitations, breakages, and shifts of our experience.

Faith is why we keep repeating the patterns of our lives. The power of faith is who we are in relationship to it. Do we fill this vessel that holds us completely? Or are we just a drop of liquid on the bottom? And if we are small inside our vessel, how do we grow and accumulate more substance by which to fill it? And what happens when we do?

Belinda said she didn't believe that. She hated the so-called faith she had learned in Germany. She didn't see the relevance of her childhood experience in her adult life. That was not – and had never been – part of who she was. I pointed to her sculpture and asked her to explain the duality of love and terror that was represented in the monster and the girl. Why were the figures intrinsically connected and inseparable? Because, I said, one cannot exist without the other, and while I agree that you do not share your father's faith, your faith is the product of your relationship with him and all that was your experience as a child in Germany. Faith is rooted in love, and because we do not choose our first loves, we are in constant reaction to them. Maybe this is why there is the ritual of baptism – to cleanse us of influence so that we may become free to exercise our will.

The terror of free will is that it allows us to tear down the walls we employ as definitions – those barriers that keep us small and contained. To live freely and unafraid of filling the vessel that is the form of our faith, we have to accept that we are the product of a union between our childhood experience and our reaction to it. We have to forgive the influence of that experience, make it fluid instead of rigid, and let it go so that we are alone in our faith and in the actions that we choose – not haunted or controlled by our past. Belinda shook her head vehemently. "I am not afraid," she said. "Look, just look at what I have done with my life. I live here. In Taos. In a different house than my husband and I don't live like my father. I live like me." If she was beyond influence, I asked her, why had she returned to Germany for two years to nurse the dying man that she hated? She said she had to, that no one else would. I nodded knowingly, like I was capable of suspending my past through forgiveness. I believed I was strong enough to exercise my will instead of my intellect and that her assertion of a life not controlled by fear was dirty with dishonesty. I was the deacon, capable of rooting it out and revealing her for what she was.

Hard tears formed behind my eyes. My stomach turned into knots and my body trembled as I looked upon my sculpture and witnessed my truth – it was there on the table, the form of my faith and the revelation of me as nothing, as empty space, as merely light contained.

Lesson 16

As you prepare to exhibit your work, remember that art is a point of engagement, an origin of process. While you are creating a work of art, you are the object of force engaged with its process. The piece reacts to and is shaped by you. When the artwork is complete, then it becomes an object and the viewer is in process – reacting to and being shaped by it. At that moment, you can no longer speak for your work. It is alive and capable of communicating for itself. Your voice is just noise in the background.

You are fortunate in that you may witness another's process and glean a different perspective on the subject of your work but you should not interfere with that process. The child, while of your womb, is now grown and your connection with it is irrelevant when it is in relationship with another. Be silent and let your work speak.

CHAPTER 16

The first part of the poem was complete in my mind and sculpting it was quick. The last three words of the stanza were finished in less than two months and the dialog in the studio jumped ahead with only momentary pauses as the words manifested themselves through sculptural form into things I recognized and understood.

Act on.
FAITH
does *NOT*
Become.

Does was fun, simple and without weight. It looked like a combination between male genitalia and an African mask. The association of the two was a little quizzical and comical. It had a great deal of movement, but didn't actually accomplish anything. I did not take the piece very seriously yet it fit in well with the other words and so I let it go.

Not was more difficult, although just as fast. I didn't know how to sculpt the absence of something. Lynn and I hated this word and, in turn, the sculpture. Belinda was gone by then. She had finished her studio in Taos and was angry with us for the conversations about faith. Our dialog had evolved and consequently excluded her. She couldn't reconcile herself with our new understanding of the word.

Become was a better work. Like an animal frozen in time, it surged with power and movement. The movement was directional and occurred only in the internal realms of the piece. The external form was still. I knew *Become*. I had spent years talking about it, and the sculpture was the consolidation of that conversation into a single object. It was gratifying to see it on the table and understand it inside myself.

"Act on. Faith does not become." I did not know what came next. There was a wealth of emotion that was documented on paper and in my head – bad poetry and romantic sentiment – and none of it hit home. I wrote of blood, night, dancing, nakedness, carnivals, drums, death, and solitude. I did not sculpt. Instead, I painted the six waxes I had completed, photographed them, and began to take them out into the world. My exhibition record filled several pages of a résumé but, for the most part, the shows were small-time affairs and did not signify an artist of note. I believed this work was good. It was the closest I had ever come to what I defined as art. For the first time, I began to call myself an artist instead of a sculptor.

Still, the journey into the world was difficult. I didn't have a clue about what to do with the poem because it was not yet complete. It had not been cast, and I could not afford the $18,000 it would take to mold the pieces, cast them into bronze, and finish them for sale. In addition, each word was part of a whole and I was unwilling to cast just one or two of them. They needed to be shown together, in exact order, and in the right space. But I never played the game the way I was supposed to and I didn't know the power players who could make it happen. I recognized I needed help and started asking for it.

People were kind. I went to a foundry and was referred to a museum director. The museum director sent me to the owner of another foundry who also served as an artist's representative and sold work in the largest art markets. He sent me to a gallery and another museum. They sent me back to where I started. Everyone liked my work, but nobody could figure out a way to show it without casting it and no one was willing to help with casting costs. Finally, an artist friend of my mother's agreed to give me a critique. He was well known and well respected and promised to be honest.

I had butterflies in my stomach on the day that Peter came to the house. My kids and I spent the morning moving furniture out of the living room and covering filing cabinets and end tables with sheets to serve as pedestals. We cleaned everything until the glass shone and the tiles glistened. Then we placed the sculptures on the pedestals, lit incense to hide the dog and cigarette smells, and closed the curtains to block the glare of the sun. I picked a few pieces of lint off the rug. I went outside to smoke. I came back in and brushed my hair. I moved the pedestals so the planes of the sculptures lined up more exactly, did a round of touch-up paint, and polished each piece. I fixed my makeup. I put on a movie for the kids and told them they had to be quiet. I waited. Finally, the dog began to bark and I looked out the window to see a grey car following my mother's truck down the driveway.

I never know what to do in moments like this. Do I walk to the car and greet people as they pull up? Do I stand on the porch or do I wait inside the house? Do I let people settle in before I offer them something to drink? You get the picture – this is why I never played the game. There are too many rules and I break them before I even know they exist.

My father had tried to teach me the importance of Southern hospitality and grace. He would spend hours in front of the mirror before he went out or people came over, even if it was just a casual occasion with friends. "Over dress or under dress, but never just dress," he told me, believing that it was important to be noticed, to stand out from the crowd, to be one's own entity, and never fall victim to what one is supposed to do. My father didn't try to fit in – he wanted people to fit to him instead. A careful combination of strong, dark eyes and laughing charisma gave him that power. To me, he was always the center of attention, emanating life and warmth. Standing or sitting, welcoming or waiting, he knew how to make people feel comfortable and glad they came. I did not.

I waited just outside the front door. When my mother and Peter came close, there were introductions, a hug and a handshake. The kids, of course, did not stay in the bedroom, and I was flustered, having lost the sophisticated environment I had sought to create in the clamor of children greeting their grandma. Peter started to grin when the kids grabbed my mother's hand and pulled her into the living room to see what we had done. They were proud of their accomplishment as they pointed out every detail – the relocated furniture, the draped sheets over the makeshift pedestals, and the just-cleaned house. They thought this was the reason for the visit. They did not know that grandma and her friend had come to view and comment upon the fabric of their mother's soul or that I wanted Peter to believe we always lived like this – in incense-filled rooms behind closed curtains, where our spotless house did double duty as a gallery. My attempt at Southern hospitality had failed thanks to the enthusiasm of my children, but as I was bemoaning this disaster in my head, Peter began to walk around the room.

My guest didn't say a word as he moved from piece to piece – circling each one before moving to the next and then starting the cycle again. As I watched him, my heart sank at his lack of response.

Wanting to break the silence and elicit a comment, I offered a round of drinks. Peter just waved his hand and shook his head. My mother accepted the offer. Once I was in the kitchen, I breathed a sigh of relief, just to be away from the heavy silence of the living room. When I returned, Peter was sitting next to my mother. I handed her the drink and finally asked him, "What do you think?" Peter took a deep breath, then said in a slow, slightly high-pitched voice, "Oh my! I'm not really sure what to think." He must have seen my face fall and my body slump because then he said, "The first thing I thought was, 'Oh My God'." He paused for a moment and stated, "They're good, Destiny. They are very, very good."

Lightness entered my body and I felt like I could fly. I had waited for such a long time to hear those words from someone of Peter's stature, and once they were spoken, I couldn't believe that they were directed toward me. Who was I to be worthy of such praise? Who was I not to be? I had worked for years to get to this point, and having arrived in it, I did not know where to go next. After this, what was left? Who could I become?

I started to talk a mile a minute about how the sculptures were words and how words corresponded to geometric shapes and symbols. I told him how hard it had been to incorporate the letters without making them so conspicuous that they would obscure the form.

I asked Peter if he had seen the letters and when he said no, I started to show him. But he stopped me and said he didn't want to know. The sculptures spoke without him knowing what they were and knowing would be a distraction. He wanted to understand them on his own terms. I told him about the relevance of the sculptures as words. I said that if people didn't know about the words, they wouldn't perceive the many layers in my work. He still said no. The sculptures said more by themselves than I could ever say for them.

We talked for a long time about the work, the casting difficulties, the number of pieces in the series, to whom I had shown the work, and what had been said in response. Then he walked around each piece again, shaking his head.

Before he left, he asked me to bring him photos of my work and if I would mind if he shared them with a few people. I hugged and thanked him, and in a voice I knew was too loud said, "No, I wouldn't mind at all." After I walked him to his car, I floated back into the house where my mother was opening windows. "It really stinks in here," she said. For a second I was mortified, and then I didn't care.

Lesson 17

U se your life. Do not use your ideas about life or even about beauty to create your work. Often our confusion about art comes from our desire to touch and express the universal. There is greatness in that quest. It provides a foundation for hope and the joy of knowing that we are not alone. But you cannot sculpt an ideal. You can only sculpt your desire. Speak honestly. Speak from the heart. Live and look at your life. But know yourself first.

CHAPTER 17

As November fell into frost-covered mornings, I struggled with the poem. Peter's appreciation for the work had given me new confidence and greater determination, but I was stuck. The words I had been playing with were melodramatic – surface wrappings for emotions I was not able to plumb. And the time of year didn't help.

I hated the holidays. Obligations, money worries, and the fear of disappointing my kids manifested in the studio as a compilation of dread and avoidance that I was not able to overcome. The business of event planning filled the space of my life. Phone conversations flew back and forth between the members of my family and voices trembled or condemned as holiday plans were made, broken, and made again.

My mother insisted on hosting Thanksgiving at her place in Pecos. She told me she had spent thirty years building a home for her kids, and by the time she had finished, we had vanished into our own lives, and she was alone. The holidays were the one time of the year that she had her family back. I couldn't argue with her. I knew her story too well. But for me, holidays at her house didn't work. It was too small for all of us and unsuited for children – they had no place to go, no games to play, no television to watch and it was usually too cold outside. I dreaded the vigilance I had to keep to avoid the constant badgering of, "Don't touch that!" or, "Not in the house!"

I was a frustrated idealist, always caught up in the fact that life did not meet my expectations and the holidays were the quintessential moment of disappointment and betrayal. Each year I remembered why I had left the bosom of my family to move to the cold, harsh environs of Boston, and each year I wished there was some way to avoid the holiday gathering that brought me back. And now that I lived here again, there was no getting around it. On Thanksgiving morning, I wrapped my pies, packed the car and drove to Pecos with my kids.

Dinner was to be at 4:00 that day – a time selected to allow everyone ample time to arrive and settle in before the meal. Mom thought we would take a hike in the early afternoon or maybe play some football in the yard. But it was freezing cold and starting to snow. No one felt much like being outside.

The house was warm with a fire in the stove and music playing. The table my father built was pulled out from the wall and neatly covered with a Turkish cloth and candlesticks. There were snacks on the table – carrots, fruit, and cranberry bread – and for a time, the seven of us crowded together in the living room sipping wine and telling stories.

Close to 3:00, my brother and his wife had still not arrived and Mom started to get a little tense. She knew they had an earlier event with his wife's family and there was a spear of jealousy edging her concern. She changed the music from soft jazz to Irish marching fare, which drowned out conversation. My kids got bored and began to wrestle with their aunt, putting dirty feet and hands all over Mom's new white sleeper sofa. Bodies, noise, and mismatched furniture filled the tiny room. Mom shot my sister a look and told me to control my kids. We hastily moved the game off the couch and onto the floor. The laughter was loud and apparently unappreciated because the dreaded, "Not in the house!" came ringing from the kitchen.

I poured another glass of wine and remembered my childhood in that living room. For years, a long, white carpet covered the floor and a green couch sat in front of the fireplace. Some nights my mother would get on her knees to play "Red light, Green Light" with us and tickle us until we screamed. On other nights, my father would play the piano while we sang and danced, or he would pretend to be a monster and we would run through the house, yelling ahead of his roars with frightened delight.

In different years in different houses, we made forts out of every piece of furniture and slung our legs loosely over the side of the sofa with drinks and chips in hand. I remembered the tarantulas, lizards, frogs, snakes, and even an owl that we collected and brought into the house without fear.

"Not in the house." I did not understand the origin of those words any more than I understood the other rules that had surfaced since I returned home. They were not the words of my childhood and I didn't recognize the voice of the woman who uttered them.

My stomach knotted as I watched the tears of my youngest about to fall. Thinking I could clear the air by getting out of the house, I bundled my children up and set out for a walk. We didn't get far, maybe a half-mile to just past the gate. But off the road and up the mountain a little way, there was a cave – my secret, childhood refuge. It was a magic place with baby stalagmites and two dark tunnels just big enough for a kid to crawl through that opened into larger rooms where bats slept. The mouth of the cave was perched on a child-sized cliff. Someone had built a ladder for easy access, which was camouflaged by the gooseberry bushes, and wild primrose that grew rampant in the small canyon beneath it. I thought we would climb into the cave, build a fire, and watch the snowfall. But as soon as we got there, we heard the sound of a truck and realized my brother and his wife had arrived. The kids thought we would miss Thanksgiving if we stayed in the cave and I knew if we did not go back to the house my mother would target her pent-up worry toward me. So we climbed down the rickety old ladder and dragged our legs through the tangled, snow-covered brambles to the road, where we raced each other toward the house.

Things were buzzing when we returned. The food that had been prepped for hours was finally on the stove and in the oven. The music had changed again to some quiet Country Western tunes, and someone had put another log on the fire. The living room had a festive mood, and I believed the brewing storm had subsided.

After the hugs and quick greetings, we settled around the table with more wine and began the usual discourse on topics of interest. My brother led the conversation, and as it deepened, it moved to a place I didn't want to go. He had read an article about educational institutions teaching values to children, and he didn't believe that any institution should take on that role. He thought it was a waste of time and money to try to instill values in school-aged children because by the time they were that old, it was too late.

I told him to be careful about what he was saying. I was trying to warn him, trying to let him know that I could not accept any inferences that my children had been ruined because of what they had experienced in the course of my marriage. His statement was the articulation of my deepest fear. He needed to stop the direction of his thoughts or I would have to confront him and demand a retraction of his voiced convictions. If I didn't face up to him on this subject, I would have to live with the knowledge that he believed I had failed as a mother and there was no hope for my children. But I did not want to argue with him – I didn't know how.

I felt that I'd lost everything I was supposed to have been or to have achieved in my life. I'd failed at marriage and endangered my kids. Based on my need for normalcy and my belief in the salvation it promised, I'd made wrong decisions. I'd come crawling to my childhood home in deep shame and mortal fear of the consequences of my actions, and I could not sit at a Thanksgiving table with my family and listen to judgment and condemnation that hit so close to the bone. I needed their approval. But the nodding heads around the table in response to my brother's declaration were the furies weaving my fate. I knew then that I would never be one of them. They would never see me or value and respect what my life had been, let alone what it was becoming. My experience and struggle to regain equilibrium and respectability, to not be a victim, and to provide a good and loving home for my kids meant nothing. I was not up to their standards of what a member of our family should be. I was trapped in who I had been.

My brother did not heed my warning. "Be careful of what?" he asked. He did not see the panic in my heart, the welling of grief and loss, or the ground turning liquid beneath me. "It's true," he said. "It's been documented. Children learn everything they will ever know about values in the first five years of their life."

I started to slide, to fall into myself, and into darkness. I clung to what I knew and needed to believe. I was impassioned as I began to talk. I was a teacher and a mother. I got paid to teach values to children whose parents neglected to do so, and I had witnessed change. It was never too late to save a child or to give children the tools they needed to save themselves.

My brother did not want to hear what I had to say. He stood up, slammed his hand on the table and said, "I don't need any more of your fucking lectures. You think you know everything about kids and art and I'm sick of it!" He left the table and stormed off into the kitchen. I ran outside and lit up a cigarette. That night, twenty years of pent-up anger spewed out of me in a ragged, wine-washed voice. My family had never loved me. I had never belonged. Existing in their own little worlds, they were judgmental, condescending, and condemned those who lived lives unlike them. They didn't know my life and they didn't know me – nor would they ever try to – because they didn't care.

It was an all-out battle that Thanksgiving Day, and when I left my mother's house the next morning, I decided not to return. I was done with family. I didn't need them. I had my own life, my children, and my friends. I paid my bills. I was respected in my job. Peter loved my work. Maybe I could not forgive my past, but I could suspend it. It wasn't welcomed in my life anymore.

Lesson 18

We often find beauty in the most frightening places. We have to look for it in the space between our memories and ideals in order to sculpt it. Rodin's sculpture, She Once was the Helmet Maker's Beautiful Wife, *demonstrates that beauty does not lie in the form of the body or the assignation of a title. To the viewer, this sad, old woman whose wrinkled skin falls away from her body like rags appears more beautiful in her old age than how she looked as a young girl simply because we did not know her then. We only see her now. And in the moment, we love her for who she is. We can imagine who she was via our own experiences with the fresh, vital bloom of young, recently married women. But our memories are frozen. They are not alive. They do not breathe.*

When you sculpt the things that frighten you, sculpt them as they are instead of how you want them to be or how you remember them. Remove yourself from the picture and let them simply be. You will then find beauty in them instead of the dictates of your desire because your work will speak to you.

CHAPTER 18

The Saturday after Thanksgiving, Lynn and I were in the studio. I told her about the holiday fiasco. I was still languishing about my decision and looking for her support. She didn't give it. Nor did she condemn me. She only said, "Destiny, at some point you are going to have to deal with grief." On that day, I did not know grief is a beautiful thing.

Grief was like falling to me. I did not know how to let myself go into the darkness of this cavernous pit. When people asked me how I was coping after my father's death, I told them I was reading James Agee's book, *A Death in the Family,* and that it helped. The words felt flat on my tongue when I uttered them though they were the only appropriate things I could think of to say. In those months following the accident, I wanted stillness. I wanted to hold onto the knowledge of a world intact. The world my father had told me about, a world full of romance and passion, was still possible through the fading smells of Old Spice and Lucky Strike cigarettes in our house.

One afternoon shortly after his death, I sat in my father's closet with the doors shut. His clothes surrounded me. They were soft, yet rough to the touch like his face in the morning. I nestled my body against his shoes and the scratchy rug, burrowing away from the light that filtered through the slats of the doors in thin, pencil-like stripes. I was alone. I wanted to stay forever in the silent scent of his belongings that brushed against me in the dark. I needed the familiar smells and textures. I needed the solitude.

Eventually, the army of visiting relatives came looking for me. They wanted me to eat. They wanted me to be okay and live in the world of daylight. When they found me crawling out of the closet, they wanted to know what I had been doing in there. I couldn't explain it to them. I did not believe they would understand.

My relatives wanted everything neat and memories out of sight. They were loud in the house and in my mind with their regular meals, grocery lists, and cheerful chatter about nothing. They appreciated the nightly gift of prepared food left on the doorstep by people who had seldom been anything but cruel. Someone cleaned the house, packed up my father's things, and sold his car. His closet was empty. We were moving back to the house in Pecos and my world did not make sense anymore.

I did not cry at my father's funeral service. I wanted to cry as much as I wanted the sky to be overcast and dark. I thought that my tears would fall silently as my body trembled. But it was a beautiful, sunny day and I couldn't cry. My face was dry and tight. I was silent. The people who came to bury him laughed when the deck we had just built sank a foot underneath the weight of their bodies. They brought food, told stories, and talked about their jobs. They strolled through the greenery around the house and walked up the dirt road admiring the wildflowers.

To me, burial was a somber thing, a punctuation mark that finalized a life. I thought if my father could see me – and I believed he could – that he would be angry and very sad because other people's lives were more important than his death and his daughter didn't cry for him. I would have if I could – and I wanted him to know that. But I never did cry for him. When finally I cried, it was only for me.

"At some point, Destiny, you are going to have to deal with grief," Lynn said. I sat in the studio twisting wax in my hands. I told her, "I do not want to deal with grief because with grief, I am alone." I spun those words over and over inside my mind, working them to loosen the knot that had formed in my stomach when I spoke. I played with the order of them. With grief, I am alone. I am alone with grief. Grief. Alone.

We talked about grief and the first stanza of the poem. I knew that the walls of faith create the form we fill and they are immutable. I also understood that we seldom let ourselves fill our form completely because we are unwilling to break down the walls that have been created for us by our experiences. I realized I had to try to fill the form of my faith. I had to move with grief into the shadows. The poem was here – in this thing about grief and being alone – but I had never allowed grief into my conscious mind. Grief was like faith – powerful and containing – and I knew what it was supposed to look like. I had seen an aunt sit Shiva for days when her husband died. I saw my mother become unhinged after my father died. I felt none of the things I observed in others. As a witness to grief, I could recognize it but I could not see it in myself.

Sitting in my father's closet on that long-ago afternoon, I had closed my eyes and allowed the feeling of grief to open. I could picture grief flowing like water. In my mind, it gathered in pools as it made its way slowly underneath locked doors and into unknown rooms. I followed and tried to stop it. I wanted to mop it up before it reached the places behind the doors. But though it was slow moving, I couldn't catch it. This silvery, expanding wet was always a little ahead of me.

By itself, grief – expanding as it was into unknown rooms – was thrilling. I envisioned a moon-like substance traveling in night, spilling out and into nothingness until nothingness was revealed as a solid thing. Like a quiet trickle under my skin, the outlines of forms became barely visible in this liquid light. I took me out of the words. Alone with grief...

I sculpted *Grief.* I had decided grief was a good and necessary thing. Sculpting it, I could embrace it willingly. I would flow with it into those dark places. But grief was heavy. I did not know how to rid the word of its weight.

I was frozen when my father died – an aspiring adolescent with huge ideas and no tools with which to implement them. I spent most of my life believing that my successes were one continuous masquerade. I felt like the great Wizard of Oz behind the curtain. I had been a child poet to please my father, and he had responded to my efforts. We spent hours together rewriting my poems, reading books, and talking about words. I always believed in the back of my mind that the poems I published and the contests I won were not entirely, even mostly, of my creation. I lived in constant fear that my curtain would be pulled aside and I would be revealed as an inspired fraud. I did not want to know grief – and neither did I want to stop the show. I was supposed to be great. But I was not great or even necessarily good. I just knew how to talk, making it up as I went along.

I recreated the image of my father through a series of relationships that allowed me to continue the masquerade. That was my grief. I held onto those relationships so as not to stand alone. I thought I would be very small by myself. I did not realize until I sculpted the word grief that the only thing I would lose would be the weight of the illusion I sought to create and the identity I wanted to assume. Conceptually, it seemed that grief might be the link between act and faith, between free will and predestination. If I could get through grief, I could perhaps forgive and then my actions might be dictated by my will instead of my desire to recreate my past.

As Lynn and I talked, the sculpture evolved and I recognized that the loss of relationship is akin to a leap of faith because it reveals the dark halls of self and opens doors to rooms of knowledge where light is seldom seen.

The decision to suspend my past and sever my relationship with my family was a self-protective move. It allowed me to continue my charade by permanently locking both myself and the members of my family into carefully controlled definitions. I saw these definitions as the walls that stopped me from filling the form of myself. The sculpture progressed.

I realized while working on it that once one has moved through grief, there is no retreat. The two primary shapes of the sculpture demonstrated that the experience of grief is a self-contained journey. The rectangle implied that the journey is safe. The circle, however, suggested that the journey is a dizzying and spiraling maze through the unknown parts of oneself. It is never ending. One can make it through the piece and get to the other side, but once there, the path only leads back to the beginning.

I could not rid grief of its weight because grief is a massive insulator. It is armor for survival. I had carried the idea of myself in the context of my relationship with my father through all the dark tunnels of my life. It was the only way I knew myself and my only method for living. By locking both myself and my family into carefully controlled definitions, I had the capability to continue my illusion. Seemingly, my family had accepted a life beyond my father. I had not. I accused them of rejecting him and who we were as a family. They accused me of denial. Each of our accusations was correct. In ceasing to allow them into my life, I found a way to make them stay in the roles and definitions I devised for them. I clung to the picture of us as the family we were when my father was alive, and I was willing to use almost any means necessary to keep that picture intact. I did know grief. Grief hid my desire for what was lost.

Lesson 19

*S*culpture is a tantric medium. As artists, we *know* sculptural expression through the silent communication of touch. However, sculpture is also a visual medium. It must present an experience that evokes sensory feelings through the eyes of the viewer so the viewer can be in the moment we are expressing instead of a witness to it.

We create sensory feelings through movement. The relationship between voluminous forms and the way light travels around the piece, coupled with its dark places and shadow lines, all work together to create movement. The more complex our work, the more intense the sensory experience. Deep caverns and bold swells are like ocean tides or intimate dancing. They create a sense of undulating movement. Quick, sharp repetitive planes inspire movement that is kin to running. Parallel planes that get bigger or smaller create directional movement and the feeling of getting somewhere, like ascending or descending a stairway. Each work must create a feeling of movement that is relevant to the experience we are trying to express. The planes that create movement must be executed with conviction so that the viewer can enter the work and experience movement both visually and emotionally. If our work does not elicit exploration and evoke an emotional response, it will simply remain pretty, decorative, and superficial.

CHAPTER 19

My children and I danced together before they were born. We danced alone through the days and nights of my marriage. Holding each other close, we danced all the way back to New Mexico. I sang loudly with the music while spinning my pregnant body around and around the room. After my children were born, the dancing continued amid tears or giggles as we swooped, bent, and swooped again. Touch, cries, and laughter were our first methods of communication. They were the sensations we trusted.

When my children were old enough to stand and talk, I changed the music from Billie Holiday, Ray Charles and Janis Joplin to Stray Cats, James Brown, and Stevie Ray Vaughan. And while we danced, I taught them how to fight. I would kneel on the carpet in the living room with my back to our big, brick fireplace. They would run at me with shining eyes and open mouths, yelling together with their little clenched fists and feet flailing.

While moving to the music, I taught them how to block an attacker, meet my eyes instead of watching my hands, and to throw their punches in rhythm. We had rules – they couldn't climb on me and they couldn't come at me from behind. If someone went down, we all had to stop until that person got up again. No hitting in the face or below the belt. We called the game, "Boom," and we played it every day, singing loudly and dancing.

I was with grief like I had been with child. I was pregnant with it, carrying its weight, and nourishing it. Grief ate from my body, altering my shape and depleting my resources. But it was a child of my creation and my responsibility. It was part of me. I would feed it, sing and dance with it. Under my care, grief would grow big enough to stand on its own or consume me completely. Then grief would be something separate from me and I would be free of its weight – free to fight it with grace and maybe laughter.

I remember dancing for my father – not with him. When I was seven, I danced with my brother on the dark, slippery floor of my father's nightclub. I wore pigtails, an ankle-length, pink-checked dress with ruffled lace on the cuffs and hem, and my patent leather shoes. My brother wore a tie. The music was slow when we walked onto the dance floor, and we were scared. We wanted to be grownups. We wanted to be beautiful and graceful in that soft light. As we began to move to the music, the other dancers stepped aside, leaving us alone. We were objects that conjured memories of lost moments and innocence for the people watching us. When the song was over, the crowd clapped and we ran back to our table. My dad ruffled my hair and smiled. He was proud. He reaped admiration from the people at our table. I did not want to sit with him. I went, instead, to hug my mother.

There were other times I danced for my father. Mostly, I danced next to the piano while he played. I don't think it ever crossed my mind to dance with him. I was his work in progress, a thing of his creation, and someone that did not really exist except to please him. I was too much aware of my pre-pubescent failings – too heavy, awkward and socially inept – to ever feel like I succeeded. I worked hard at correcting my flaws and being who I was supposed to be. I dieted when he said I was fat. I matched my shorts to the colored band on my bobby socks. I parted my hair to the side the way he liked it and cursed my reflection when the part wouldn't stay because my hair parted naturally in the middle. I read the books he assigned me and made the grades in school. I was a terror on the soccer field because I was supposed to be the best, to never get tired, and to suck up injuries. I showed him my poetry but hid my journals.

With my children, I did not lose my sense of myself as an individual. That distinction made it possible for me to dance with them, rather than for them. The relationship transformed an environment that was heavy and cold into one that was rich with beauty and laughter. I could also dance with grief and, by extension, with my father. It was time for me to move in rhythm with him. He was, after all, no more or less human than I. By dancing with him, I could know him differently and see myself as separate from him. And if I held him close, I would not be victim to his watching eyes.

Act on!
Faith
Does Not
Become.

With Grief,
Alone,
Dance

I knew the first part of the second stanza and sculpted the words quickly. *With* was an expression of metamorphosis. *Alone* was tiny and almost joyous. Although dwarfed in comparison to *With* and *Grief*, it seemed charming, simple, and elegant. For the first time in my life, alone was not the emphasis or determining factor in my decision-making process. I could see it for what it was – diminutive, without weight, and unencumbered. I could hold it in the palm of my hand. I felt good about the piece. It was not frightening.

A door opened. My feeling of grief did not have to be a block or the impediment to my will. *Alone* was not scary and *With* was beautiful. I was ready to sculpt *Dance* and move through my own grief. *Dance* could transform my grief into mourning.

I invited my family to spend Christmas day at my house. Knowing this was risky business, I also invited some friends to act as a buffer. My intent was to repair some of the damage that had been done. Surprisingly, my family was gracious and formal as they politely conversed with others. We didn't drink very much. I kept my distance by smoking cigarettes in the studio. The kids had a place to play and did not roughhouse in the living room. We were all on our best behavior. After dinner they left with generous thanks. I was grateful they had come, yet relieved they had gone. I loved them. I would have to work hard at creating a new model for our relationship that didn't revolve around my feeling of being watched, scrutinized, and judged. In addition, I would have to dance with them – moving with them in my heart, not in my mind, and in the present instead of the past.

Two days later, I got a phone call from a prestigious contemporary gallery. Peter had showed them photographs of my work, and the owner was willing to come out to the studio to see the word series.

I wanted to sculpt *Dance* and move through the stanza to another perspective and way of living. I wanted to hold my father, my family and my lost childhood close in the intense, undulating rhythm of my life. I wanted to feel alive, sexy and in motion, rather than being awkward, stilted, and judged. I needed to embrace the love instead of the loss. I had been given a chance. But this sculpture would have to wait.

We set up an appointment for the third week in January and I went to work. The series was good but it could be better. To make matters worse, some pieces had partially melted in the heat of the garage. Some were scratched or gouged due to cats, children, and my own carelessness in shuffling them around. I never got back to resolving the problems with *Not*. The sculptures were dark. I didn't have pedestals and filing cabinets would be less than appropriate for this viewing. One by one, I went through the pieces again, striving for perfection. I also prayed for a thick, white blanket of snow to cover my bare, brown yard.

Lesson 20

Dancing is a wonderful experience, but you cannot dance all the time. The intensity of movement in a work is vital to bringing a viewer into the experience. It can also be overwhelming, causing the viewer to turn away from the piece before ever becoming involved. This is why you cannot merely suggest your primary shapes through negative space. You will have to sculpt some of their lines. This will allow access to the form and create places for the viewer to rest inside it. If you are sculpting parallel and repetitive planes to take your viewer somewhere, you need to be sure they will get there. That means you have to make room for broad planes and create breathing spaces in your work.

Like with light and shadow, movement and places of rest must work with each other in dialog or one will dominate the other. You are looking for balance in your expression because there is balance in life. Even when you are caught up in the frenzy of making love, there are momentary pauses in a caress or a kiss that allow you to find yourself in time and space. Without those intermittent moments one would find it difficult to be vulnerable and open to the experience. We cannot lose ourselves in our experience. Nor can your viewers entirely lose themselves in the experience of your work. A place of rest will create opportunity for the viewers to feel certain about your expression and see themselves in relationship to it.

CHAPTER 20

There was a time when I believed in what I felt – walls were solid things, I was alive to my experience and too young to question it. There were rich smells and warm touches. On summer afternoons, big pine trees turned black in the rain and aspens swayed with yellow grasses, their outlines blurred and blended like a soft watercolor. Crouched and shivering, big drops of water fell on my head from the branches of the tree. I would wait and count the seconds between lightning and thunder to see if it was safe to run across the field and into the house where there was a fire in the stove, welcoming voices, and maybe hot chocolate.

Something inside me had changed. I did not know what. I couldn't believe that the repetition of experience had shaped my body into this slouch. Nor did I understand why I had waited all those years for an axe to fall – shattering my world and beckoning night to descend. As a child, terrible nights had come all the time. My mother said I had too strong of a will. I'd never had a chance to ask my father why he'd chased me around the green couch with his belt while my mother watched through the kitchen window. I remember the chase and my father's voice, but not what happened when he caught me.

The nights came and the nights went. When morning came, I did not live in fear or dread; I did not hunch my body against expected onslaught, or tense my muscles in anticipation. During the day, I did not believe that I would have to pick up the broken shards of my life and glue them together again with the desperate determination of my will. I took what came and woke again to cool mornings and the sound of water under a bridge. Slipping on a dress, I ran to the bridge with my plastic tea set, stuffed animals, and Mrs. Peabody doll. I believed the day would stay brightly decorated by the songs I made up as the tall grass tickled my shins.

When I was little, I had been capable of moving through my days and nights without questioning or hating them. Now, I wanted to live in that part of myself again and believe there would come another time when I would sit casually in a chair and take in the silence of a winter world. I needed to breathe deep, move slowly, and touch someone without wondering if the touch was real. I wanted to remember how to trust and forget about my battles with languages, walls, and definitions. I was ready to simplify my world, live gently, and believe again in what I felt.

The gallery owner arrived at precisely 10:07 on the morning of January 28. It snowed the night before, but the snow had since melted and the yard was muddy. My kids were at school, my house was quiet, and I was ready. The sculptures – painted with colored wax to look like bronze – were in the studio, mounted on borrowed pedestals.

We talked briefly over coffee. She explained that she wasn't taking on new artists at this time, but because Peter had been so impressed with my work she felt she owed it to him to see it and offer me advice. I told her about the casting problem. The works needed to be cast and shown together. She told me most that artists cast one or two pieces at a time and when those sell, they cast more. I agreed with her and told her I had done that in the past, but this work was different. When the coffee was halfway down in my cup, I invited her to see the sculptures.

There was a small step leading from the house into the studio. I cautioned her as I opened the door, prompting her to look down to her feet. Then she looked up and froze with one foot in the studio and the other still in the living room. She put her coffee down on the washing machine and stepped fully into the room, exclaiming, "Oh Wow!" Then she began to walk around the words. I steered her to the beginning – to *Act* and *On*. There was an order she needed to follow, a specific way of seeing the works that would allow her to discover the relationships between them. In this order, the works would speak for themselves.

Recalling my experience with Peter, I pulled up a chair and waited. I watched her gently touch the pieces, one by one. With raised eyebrows, she turned her head in quick starts as if she had seen something that might vanish if she looked too hard. "Peter said something about them being words," she remarked. I nodded my head and stood. I brought her back to *Act* and began to tell the story, pointing out the letters as I spoke. Her eyes and hands followed the form, before moving to the next word. She asked about *Faith* and *Become* as she lingered again over each one. Then she began to talk.

Her immediate questions were whether or not anyone else had seen my work, were there other galleries interested, and had any been sold? She told me she had dreaded coming out to see this work. When Peter told her about the words, she had expected another gimmick from a flaky Santa Fe artist. She couldn't believe how good the sculptures were. Then she said she would do a show, but a different kind of show. She wanted to exhibit the works in wax and give collectors an opportunity to buy the work for the cost of casting them in bronze. Then, after they were sold, we would do another show the following year. The deal would be that the collectors had to loan back the works after they were cast so we would have a complete set of bronzes to show.

"How many will there be in the series?" she asked. I told her I wasn't quite sure. I knew there would be at least twelve but there could be as many as fourteen. She talked about dates, what she would need and when. She would send out her photographer to do a shoot. Other considerations that she rattled off included press releases, colors, the fragility of the wax, pricing, and marketing strategies. She talked about a tour through Colorado and San Francisco. She had some museum friends that would help. The work could travel for six months and then come back for the big show. "Peter was right," she said. "He was absolutely right."

She hugged me when she left and promised we would talk soon. I let the dog out of the bedroom and watched her back down the driveway. I was going to have a show at the gallery of my dreams. I poured another cup of coffee, lit a cigarette, and started making phone calls. Strangely, I was not overly excited. There was a sense of certainty in my body, a feeling like coming home. In that given moment, everything was as it should be.

I tried for days to understand what was different about this meeting. There was no roller coaster of up-and-down emotions. I did not feel frenzy. I hadn't spoken for the works or tried to sell the woman my ideas. She loved them anyway. Somewhere deep inside, I knew this series would be a success. Their creation and the events that followed were almost beyond my control. The entire process had consumed me for months and I was exhausted. One sculpture followed another and the subsequent events had overwhelmed me. I needed to rest and not get emotionally caught up in this experience. The gallery owner's reaction was the culmination of years of effort, and I wanted to stop here and be still. Her excitement was enough for the both of us. She could take the ball and run with it because all I needed to do was work on *Dance*.

When Lynn came out on Saturday we decided to hire an assistant. There was too much work for the both of us and we needed to keep sculpting. For the first time, I was willing to let go of the technical aspects of the work. I didn't need to dress the waxes or clean up those tight spaces that prohibited the use of tools. The forms were there. The planes were clearly defined. Someone else could do this work and more. There were molds to be made, bronzes to be chased, and patinas to be applied. Lynn and I wanted to create. She was determined to have a body of work by spring of that year and I had a show to prepare. We could not afford to be stuck in the tedium of detail.

We talked about the kind of person we wanted and agreed that whoever we hired needed to fit into the studio dynamic. This person would have to be able to engage in the dialog and have enough skills to work independently. The assistant would also have to be trustworthy, good with kids – or at least tolerant of them – flexible in schedule, and willing to work for $8 an hour. We wrote a help-wanted notice and laughed at ourselves. It would be a miracle if we found the person so-described.

We waited for weeks with no responses to our ad. One woman called to inquire about classes and we interviewed her. She was allergic to smoke, so we ruled her out. We let the idea of an assistant go by the wayside and concentrated on sculpting.

Lesson 21

Do not confuse resolution with revelation. Resolution is the process of reducing a complex idea into a smaller, more manageable form. In sculpture, we begin with a question. We move through a process trying to balance light and shadow, geometric forms, negative and positive space, areas of movement, and areas that are still so as to frame our question and form a context for understanding. Our attempt to resolve our question and find an answer creates opportunity for revelation.

Revelation is the product of honest expression. Divine truth can only come from honesty. No matter how great our attempt to resolve our question, we will not experience revelation until we listen to what our work is trying to tell us. We must let go of our need for control in order for truth to be revealed. Our work gives us perspective. It provides us with access to what we think and feel and helps us see beyond the veil of our immediate knowledge. If you only try to resolve the question, you will not recognize the revelation. Do not settle for resolution and control. Be willing to grow with your work. As you grow, so too will it.

CHAPTER 21

I love to watch the fluid, undulating movement of danc-ers. They are ephemeral and not grounded to the earth like me. I imagined my sculpture for *dance* would be similar – graceful and vertical, a whirling pirouette suspended in time. I carved the letter D, put it on a board, and began to build – placing letters on top of each other in a staggered stack. I didn't like what I saw.

The sculpture was clumsy and stiff like a big-eyed, thick-legged girl with little flowers on her dress and flat, stringy hair. No one would want this dance. I did not want this dance. I wanted to move through the air – effortlessly and with beauty.

Lynn's piece wasn't working either. She had decided to sculpt her relationship to God. She put herself in the mid-dle of the composition and worked on building three fig-ures around her. The first figure was dark, reaper-like, and menacing. The second was apathetic, simply a witness. The third was an angel, nurturing and tender. The three figures were disconnected, while the figure of Lynn was hunched, self-conscious, and afraid.

Lynn talked about failure. She thought she might go back to painting watercolors and put sculpture on hold for a while. Having pursued sculpture for almost three years, she felt nothing had been accomplished. Her slide entries to shows had all been rejected. She hadn't sold anything. "I don't have the kind of time you do," she said when I argued with her. "I don't have ten years. I don't even have five years and it costs too much money. I need a break, a different perspective. Maybe I'm not supposed to be an artist. Maybe I should just be happy with what I have and let art be a hobby."

Recalling the scene, *Dance* loomed over Lynn's piece as we worked side by side at the long, particleboard table. Stubbed-out cigarettes stuck to the wax-covered floor. Empty beer bottles were strewn about. We were missing tools. The constant work, dirty studio, winter skies, muddy yards, and morning ice on the windows were too much. February had frozen our dialog. It seemed we worked for hours every Saturday and got nowhere.

I did not believe Lynn's frustration was about time or money. I thought it might be about me. About that time, Lynn and I spent an evening with two friends in a hot tub. It was a clear and bitterly cold night. New Mexico stars and too much wine inspired the four of us to shed our bathing suits and sit naked in the steaming water. While strands of our hair froze to the deck beside the discarded suits, we talked about vulnerability and a question came up. "If you could expose your vulnerability right now, about anything, what would you say?" Choosing my words carefully, I told my friends that vulnerability was about being willing to cry. If I started, I was afraid I would not be able to stop. The other women took my lead and answered casually, not really exposing too much about themselves. Vulnerability was an idea, something we talked about in therapy or aspired to in our art. It was not something we would ever be because vulnerability was feminine and dangerous. We could not afford it in our lives.

Lynn paused when the question came to her. She had been silent through our modest disclosures and now she was still. "I would tell my mother that I am a lesbian," she finally said. We were shocked. Truth hovered in the air like our cold breath. Wanting to release the pressure, I searched for something to say and came upon the forgiving nature of motherhood. Her mother would understand. She would love her daughter anyway. Lynn didn't say a word. She just shook her head and started to cry. In unison, my friends and I moved toward her. We held her close against our naked bodies. Our arms formed a protective circle around her. Our bodies said, "We love you." Yet I was angry too. Not only had Lynn spoken a truth and risen above the pseudo-intellectual game we were playing, she divulged a truth about herself that I did not know. She had betrayed me by not giving all of herself to our studio dialog.

It was not a revelation that Lynn was a lesbian. She had been out since I knew her. I just didn't know she hadn't told her mother, or that she was capable of consciously hiding her truths. That night, I recognized there were probably many things about her I did not know. She hadn't proclaimed her capacity or need to lie and that had made me a fool. She knew everything about me.

And so we were stuck, quiet around each other and hard with our sculptures – the shaping and carving of them were forceful and sharp. Lynn's piece about her relationship with God was based on the hot tub event. That night had changed her life. She had never felt so supported or loved. Her shame was retreating as she experienced the revelation that hiding is not as safe as speaking the truth. She could finally feel what she had proclaimed from the analytical side of her mind. But she was having a hard time sculpting it and I did not want to help.

Her public disclosure left me cold. Not only had she spoken it outside the intimacy of our conversations, she was ready to quit sculpting and leave me alone in the studio – in my mind and in myself. We needed fresh energy and a way to see more than the tired reflections of ourselves in each other. Had we been lovers, we would have taken a trip or gone on a date. If we were only friends, we could have gone shopping or to the movies. We were more like accomplices, trapped in a dirty hideout on a lonely mountain.

I could not believe it when a studio assistant dropped out of the sky. Greg called my office to inquire about a job in an after-school program and had experience working with kids. He also had experience with mold-making and basic sculpting concepts. He was a philosophy major at a local college. I wasted no time inviting him to interview with Lynn and me on Saturday.

Greg was perfect for our needs. He understood the technical criteria. He was flexible, willing to work for the money we could pay, and as a philosophy student he was more than capable of keeping up with the dialog. My kids would love him because he knew magic tricks and liked to laugh. It took all of ten minutes to offer him the job and he started work that day.

I didn't have much for Greg to do, so Lynn started him on the mold-making process for a piece she was getting ready to cast. She taught him about chasing the wax and explained how to block negative space in the interior of the sculpture with clay so the mold would separate when it was done. I was still fighting with *Dance* and dealing with frustration.

Lynn had never taught sculpting technique and still thought of herself as my student. She was nervous about instructing Greg and repeatedly called me over to offer assistance. I answered her questions abruptly, thinking that she wasn't willing to assume responsibility for knowing the answers herself. Late in the day, as we were getting ready to quit, Lynn said I should explain my shape theory to Greg. I had just purchased a bottle of good scotch and suggested we have a drink to celebrate our new assistant and everyone agreed. As we drank, I quickly took Greg through the shape test. My impatience was getting the best of me and I didn't allow enough time for Greg to discover the information for himself. We had another round of drinks.

When Greg asked me what I meant about body language being the same as shape language, I asked him to stand while I faced him in a fighting stance. Giggling nervously, he stepped away from me. "Stop there!" I said. Suddenly, the smile left his face as I pointed out the shape of his body in reaction to my aggressive tone. He was slightly hunched, his arms were fully extended, and his hands were crossed. He had set one foot behind the other and his head was bent downward. His posture spoke submission. It was an oval – vulnerable and non-threatening. I told him that body language is our first method of expression as we react to our experience and asked him to move toward me in an aggressive manner. He refused, so I asked Lynn to demonstrate. She looked at me like I was insane, but she stood and dutifully took a fighting position. I pointed out the angularity of her limbs and posture – all triangles, squares, and hard edges. Then I asked her to throw a punch. She shook her head and said, "I'm not going to fight you."

"This is just a demonstration," I explained, and threw a few fake punches her way. She wasn't biting. Despite Lynn's refusal to play along – even for the sake of education – I became more aggressive and asked Greg to identify the shapes as I moved. Lynn, on the other hand, sat back down and offered to pour a third round of drinks. Greg took his cue and told us he had to be getting home but he would see us next Saturday. After he had gone, Lynn asked me what I had been thinking. She wanted to know if I had gone crazy. I felt that maybe I had.

I wanted to fight. I wanted to feel the physical impact of my body on something – or someone – to know that I was real, and to be more than a mind and a whirling confusion of emotion. I knew what a punch was. I didn't have to question it a thousand times to get its meaning. I could explore my motives for hitting, but the physical act was a separate thing. It was a process of winding up, letting go, and then feeling a rush of piercing pain that needed no explanation. The motives were irrelevant because they lived in a different time. The punch was all about now, in this instant, and it was enough. Fighting put me on solid ground.

I was turning off the wax pots and tidying the worktable when the phone rang. It was Lynn's partner. She had called to make sure that Lynn was safe because she was not yet home and it was getting late. I watched Lynn hang up the phone and waited for an explanation. The expression on her face was twisted and her body looked defeated. She told me that her partner wanted to know if the two of us were having an affair. Lynn suggested we have another drink.

I was furious. Lynn did not immediately engage her partner and defend herself or proclaim my virtue. Without emotion, she simply said that she would be home in awhile. That was not good enough. What Lynn and I had was beyond petty jealousy. It was a meeting of minds and a special bond that enabled us to pursue our passions honestly. I did not understand how Lynn could so blandly accept her partner's accusation. The time we shared was sacred and worth defending.

Lynn did not agree. She said she recognized how her partner could be jealous based on the amount of time she and I spent together and the intensity of our relationship. But I believed her partner's insecurities would only be perpetuated given Lynn's refusal to defend the accusation, let alone our working relationship. I told her she was chicken not to stand up for herself and this was another example of her unwillingness to engage or confront her life directly. Her response to her partner was just like what she had done in the studio that day. Lynn did not want to take responsibility for her actions. She held her emotions back and tried to placate every situation. She abdicated power to gain control by manipulating those around her with constant declarations of, "I can't," "I won't," and, "It doesn't matter."

I fought her for the first time that night. It wasn't a raging battle and it wasn't a lucid declaration of feeling.

My fight was a drunken outpouring and an expression of fear. I was afraid of myself because I couldn't value or respect Lynn's choices. I did not want her to be a coward in her life. I believed she could be more self-confident and express the truth when need be. She was capable of courage.

I looked at her and wanted to strangle her. But she wouldn't fight me – not physically and not with words – and that made me crazy. Letting all my guards down, I was ready to give her a jolting shove and force her into some kind of action that would either free me of my responsibility for her or make her my equal. But she would not be moved. Lynn did not want to be a true colleague in every sense of the word. She was not ready to progress to a new way of living her life.

Every time I thought about her behavior in the studio or on the phone with her partner, I got angrier. I yelled and cried and tried to get her to understand what was wrong with her. I talked faster and pushed harder. She was immutable. And then I didn't know what to do – because I loved her.

Lynn was the person who helped me clearly comprehend what I was saying. She was as strong as she was weak. She was close to me even while she kept her distance. I hated that her intelligence didn't prevent her from making bad choices or living in fear. My mind said she was wrong, a coward, and a failure in life. My heart said I didn't want to lose my friend. My past history told me that there was no reconciliation between the two. I had believed in fighting for what I wanted, but my fighting failed.

We hugged when she left that night, but I expected our relationship to be over. I lay in bed worrying that she would not make it home. I envisioned a myriad of car crashes and anticipated the telephone ringing, where a voice on the other end would tell me my best friend was dead. The call did not come and eventually it was morning. Lynn called me before breakfast, told me she loved me, and she would see me on Saturday. I was stunned. Until that moment, I never knew what it meant to forgive.

Lesson 22

*A*rt is the process of relationship. Through art we create and share ourselves.

CHAPTER 22

Nearly twenty years ago, on a cool summer evening in the mountains of northern New Mexico, I stood at my father's headstone reading his epitaph. I wanted to feel something. I needed to grieve. I failed to cry when we shoveled the earth over his ashes earlier that day. The sound of dry dirt hitting metal left me blank inside, frozen and unworthy. I held his cigarettes in my hand – a crumpled pack of Lucky Strikes collected from his pockets at the scene of his death – and searched for his face in my memory. I could not find it. What echoed in my mind were the slouched body, dripping bile, and the stink of sudden death under a hot sun.

The ephemeral blue-gray of twilight sky met the jagged tops of dusk-colored pine trees far above the darkening valley in which I stood. There were crickets and creek noises that punctuated the silence and warm, yellow lights inside the windows of the house that bade me stay outside. In the cold and coming dark, away from the normal sounds of people talking as they prepared a meal, I thought I would feel the spirit of my father. I trusted that a connection with him would somehow stop me from being lost and from knowing that I was hard, unfeeling, and forever locked inside myself.

I lit one of his cigarettes. And with that first drag, I choked a little. I watched the smoke spiral up, ghostlike into the sky, and told myself that I would find him in the smoke and ash of his tobacco on fire in my hand.

The spring before my big show, I was still smoking and trying to name the ache I felt on that faraway night. I found myself thinking about that joyous little girl in patent leather shoes, unafraid and unconcerned. Instead, I was finding that the same elements were always present, regardless of who I was with or what I was doing. Striving for connection, discordant rhythms and moments persistently blurred the hard definitions of my world. I was always reaching toward an idea about what life was supposed to be, as if I was rooted in this earth only temporarily. I believed if I worked hard enough and intensified my awareness of others and myself, I would escape my bondage and truly fly.

I had been sculpting what I knew of dance from the perspective of a witness, not listening closely enough to my work to realize that watching dance is very different from actually dancing. From the sidelines, I was aware of everything surrounding the dancers – other people, background noises, lighting, and their combined forms spiraling up and away from the hard lines of earth. They appeared separate from it all, as if they were the only thing that existed and were completely free.

In the act of dancing, however, partners respond to each other's movements, generating a rhythm of give and take. Their movement is not vertical. It is horizontal, because dancing occupies the now. There is no past or future when you move in rhythm with someone – bodies are close and you share the air between you. There are only two components: interaction and synchronicity. Past and future come into play when someone moves out of step and the focus is lost. Time is merely a product of our minds and an expression of our perspective. I could not just witness the dance.

If I were to dance with my father and my husband, my children and my mother, as well as my brother, sister, and friends, I needed to dance with them now. I would have to be a finely tuned instrument and respond to the rhythms of today. I could not be striving for or stretching toward connection. I had to feel it, live it, and trust in what I felt at any given moment. Only then would the dance be real.

There was a day on which I saw the whole dance, even as I lived it. My brother's wife was pregnant and due at anytime. I was at a volunteer luncheon and the guest speakers were young men who were mountain climbers. One of them presented a talk and slide show about their experience together in the Himalayas. He started off slowly describing the trip to Tibet and the surrounding villages. He showed images of their base camp, which consisted of army trucks, tents, and necessary gear. They were happy in those pictures – smiling and waving at the camera. The slides continued to document their journey up the mountain and then the speaker put his remote control down. A close-up of a snow covered mountain face against a cold blue sky filled the screen. He described how he had lost his ice axe and said, "I should have known then that something was wrong."

He was developing edema. He had taken off his gloves to relieve himself, but when done had inadvertently put on different and less-insulated gloves. His hands froze. Still, he decided to keep climbing, for it was easier to go up and over than it was to retreat from the mountain. Because his hands were frozen, he could not undo his pants again. Urine leaked into his boots and froze his feet. Fifty feet from the top of the mountain, he wanted to die. He could not go further. His friend had reached the summit and was calling to him. After hours of trying to move just an inch, he gave up and prayed for death. His friend came down from the peak, found him in no condition to advance, and together they worked their way back down the mountain. They slid for thousands of feet as their momentum propelled them over canyons and cliffs.

On their last night – frozen and dying – they finally saw the lights of their base camp, but the speaker confessed he was defeated and had given into death. He would not go on. He sat down on a rock and waited to die. His friend left him behind in an effort to get to camp for help. The story went on and on, but in the end they survived. After they came off the mountain, their team stopped in a small village for directions to the nearest hospital. Their limbs had thawed and infection had set in. On a stroke of good luck, two hitchhikers knocked on their van hoping for a ride. The hitchhikers turned out to be doctors specializing in infectious diseases.

The speaker stopped to take a drink of water and, until that moment, I had not noticed his hands. They looked like boxing gloves – swollen mitts with protruding thumbs. He grasped his water bottle with lobster-like claws. His hands were an abhorrent, mutated mockery of the human body.

He did not blush. He did not try to hide them. He said he was done with hospitals for a while. After more than a dozen surgeries, he still had a bit of infection in one of his thumbs. He wanted to stop now and simply live. He wanted to be an artist and ride his horses.

We sat in silence when he finished. We were crying. But I felt no pity for him. His story was that of a journey, not up a mountain, but inside himself. After a few minutes he started to fidget. Still no one moved. No one clapped. No one said anything. Finally, his friend who was sitting in the audience – the one who had been with him on the mountain and lost his limbs to save a life – stood on prosthetics and said, "The soul is a difficult and fragile thing." The two of them met on stage and embraced each other. Eventually we could move but we did not stay and network. We did not go to shake their hands. We filed out to the parking lot and I heard someone ask, "Did they tape that? I sure hope they taped it."

I was reeling. I couldn't even begin to describe what I was feeling. But I had a meeting to attend and I was late. My cell phone rang just after I arrived. One of my staff was calling to find out if I knew the whereabouts of my sister-in-law's sister; it was an emergency. I hadn't a clue. Then my call waiting beeped. It was my brother. I asked him if the baby was coming and he said no. He told me that his wife's father had just died.

In that instant, the world went red. I could see it, all of it. It was a bloody ocean of ups and downs, waves that crashed against each other forming valleys and swells. Everything was connected. It all made sense. I just hadn't seen it before. I took the rest of the day off, called Lynn and met her for a Guinness. I talked with her about the baby, the death, the mountaineers, and my upcoming show. We talked about friendship. I told her I might be ready to love someone again.

On the following Saturday, I knocked *Dance* off its board and turned it sideways. Immediately, I saw again the waves, swells, valleys, and blood in a cacophony of movement and relationships. I had found a metaphor for me and my process. With grief, alone, I dance in time.

EPILOGUE

I finished the first draft of this book in 2001. Shortly after its completion, I lost my job with the youth program. September 11 had wiped out a large portion of our funding and my position had been cut. It was a terrifying time. The ensuing recession, the eerie silence of the skies, and the state of shock that permeated everything and everyone were a backdrop to my own personal crisis. I did not know how I would pay the mortgage or feed my children.

The crisis became my catharsis and was directly responsible for forcing me to take a leap into my art. It was a now or never moment. To pay the bills, I took on contract work doing molds and waxes for other sculptors. I became a full-time artist.

One of my clients was a petite, seventy-year old woman who worked in steel. She was my inspiration – I figured if she could weld, so could I. I rented some oxy/acetylene tanks and pulled out the torches, hoses, and gauges I had bought at a garage sale years before. Slowly, I taught myself how to weld. I learned how to texture the metal by trying to cover up my mistakes and I played with patina on steel even though everyone I talked with said it couldn't be done. It can.

Over the next several years, I spent countless hours in my studio and on the road driving my work to juried art fairs across the country. I learned how to talk about my work. I got stronger, my welding got better and the work sold. Eventually, galleries started to represent me and corporations and civic institutions acquired my work.

I found love again. The man in my life is exceptional – warm, generous, intelligent, and supportive. We still live in Santa Fe. My children are struggling as young adults in much the same way I did at their age, and they are beautiful. I made peace with my family and over the years, our shared history has informed, enhanced, and enriched our shared present. I consider my mother and siblings among my closest friends.

In all this time, there never has been a place of rest. I don't seem to be capable of a quiet life. There is always the next project, the new idea, and the battle against the status quo. At present, I work both as a full time artist and managing partner of La Tienda at Eldorado – a commercial complex committed to community and to promoting an environment that supports artists as much as it supports the work they produce. We sponsor a free exhibit space, a performance space, and a multitude of events that encourage dialog across a diverse range of people and artistic media.

For me, the process of relationship and the process of art are ever intertwined and the dance never ends. Years after I stopped teaching, I bumped into one of my former students. We talked for a long time about grief. For her, grief is not about loss. It's about what you didn't get. I disagree. Grief is not about what you didn't get. It is about what you didn't give.

ACKNOWLEDGEMENTS

My deepest thanks go out to all of the people who helped make this book possible. My editor, Doug, was absolutely invaluable. Without his methodical, humorous and profound insights, the book may never have seen the light of day. My friend Lindsay read more drafts over the years than anyone else and was always there to talk about whatever consumed me at the moment. Steve spent countless hours reading, listening, talking and holding me while I relived this story again and again. There are so many others who helped to make this book possible – by reading and critiquing, sharing their own stories, and giving insight and advice – that I cannot list them all here. You know who you are. Know also how much I appreciate your time, talents and friendship.

Above all, I am deeply grateful to the family and friends with whom I shared this journey. Without you, and all the beautiful and difficult times we endured, I would not be who I am today. I will never be able to tell you how much I value who you are and what you have given me.

Finally, my deepest love and appreciation go to my mother. Through her courage, wisdom and enduring love, I eventually found my own.

46072421R00132

Made in the USA
Charleston, SC
10 September 2015